Endorsements

"I needed this book. I was running on empty trying to meet others' expectations of me. Geri helped me diagnose my situation and gave me practical, applicable, biblical ways to address it. Thank you, Geri. This is a must-read. It is freeing!"

—RUTH GRAHAM, author

"I read Geri Scazzero's book on a day that had been particularly challenging—one of those "I can't handle another thing!" kind of days. I was able to listen to her wisdom without all the defensive barriers I might normally erect when I don't want to be faced with uncomfortable truth. Geri's words encouraged me—and even pushed me—to examine my patterns of relating to God and to those closest to me. Her example of living in the freedom that comes from being confident of God's love inspires me to do some intentional soul work. Thank you, Geri."

—KAY WARREN, executive
director, HIV/AIDS Initiative,
Saddleback Church

The Emotionally Healthy Woman

EIGHT THINGS
You Have to Quit to
CHANGE YOUR LIFE

Previously published as *I Quit!*

Geri Scazzero

WITH PETER SCAZZERO

ZONDERVAN®

WILLOW
Willow Creek Resources

ZONDERVAN.com/
AUTHORTRACKER
follow your favorite authors

ZONDERVAN

The Emotionally Healthy Woman
Copyright © 2010 by Peter Scazzero and Geri Scazzero

Previously published as *I Quit!*

This title is also available as a Zondervan ebook. Visit www.zondervan.com/ebooks.

This title is also available in a Zondervan audio edition. Visit www.zondervan.fm.

Requests for information should be addressed to:

Zondervan, *Grand Rapids, Michigan 49530*

This edition: ISBN 978-0-310-32001-2 (softcover)

Library of Congress Cataloging-in-Publication Data

Scazzero, Geri.
    I quit!: stop pretending everything is fine and change your life /
Geri Scazzero with Peter Scazzero.
        p.   cm.
    Includes bibliographical references.
    ISBN 978-0-310-32196-5 (softcover)
    1. Christian life. 2. Conduct of life. 3. Success — Religious aspects —
Christianity. I. Scazzero, Peter, 1956- II. Title.
BV4501.3.S287   2010
248.4 — dc22   2010005929

Published in association with Helmer Literary Services.

Cover design: John Hamilton Design
Cover photography: Yuji Sakai / Getty Images®
Interior design: Beth Shagene

Printed in the United States of America

14 15 16 17 /DCI/ 21 20 19 18 17 16 15 14 13 12 11 10 9 8

To Maria, Christy, Faith, and Eva,
that you might know, in your inmost being,
the love of Christ that is better than life

Contents

Acknowledgments

This book would not have been written without my husband, Pete. I am a ponderer. He is a writer. Although I am the one who identified, named, and articulated the skeleton of eights "I Quits" in *The Emotionally Healthy Woman*, he is the one who insisted, "You have a whole book in you." *The Emotionally Healthy Woman* reflects our team effort from the beginning to the end. It reflects what we both learned on this missing aspect of spiritual formation over a seventeen-year period.

Pete is a uniquely wonderful person whom I was so lucky to marry. One of Pete's most attractive qualities is his humility and openness to learn, grow, and change. He has always been responsive to my "Quits" and eagerly applied them to his own life. We also know how very, very blessed we are to enjoy the ongoing experience of growing together in this wonderful journey we now label "emotionally healthy spirituality." I cherish this wonderful gift that we remain on a similar learning curve after twenty-eight years of marriage.

I belong to two significant communities that have impacted my life beyond measure. The first is my extended family of parents, siblings, in-laws, nieces, and nephews, which has always been a place of connection, belonging, and love. You keep me rooted in the nonnegotiable value and support of family. You have given me a tremendous legacy for which I am eternally grateful. I would not have had the "goods" to quit if it were not for what you deposited into me.

I want also to thank my other community—New Life Fellowship Church. I am a transformed person out of our many years together. You have allowed us to pioneer new pathways of spiritual formation. We have trusted and loved each other for a quarter of a century. Thank you for being the kind of church that embraces the truths expressed in *The Emotionally Healthy Woman*.

I want to also thank Sandy Vander Zicht and Zondervan, especially for their patience in waiting on my "no pressure" schedule to write the book and for the outstanding editing on Sandy's part. Thank you, Kathy Helmers, for representing this message on my behalf.

Thank you, Barbara and Chris Giamonna, for your friendship and feedback, along with your love for the church of Jesus Christ.

Thank you, Doug Slaybaugh, for your vision and leadership for this message and your timely entrance into our lives a few years ago. And thank you, Lisa Keyes, for your initiative and perseverance in the projects around the relaunching of this book.

Finally, I want to thank my "angels" from the Midwest,

who handed me an "oxygen mask" when I was suffocating. Your generous hospitality and provision of our needs at critical junctures in our ministry here in New York City enabled me to get oxygen to my soul and persevere during those first ten difficult years. God brought many gifts of sustenance through you. I am not sure I would still be in New York without your kindnesses.

Foreword

The most loving thing Geri ever did for me was to quit the church I pastor. Yes, a part of me wanted to kill her for the humiliation I felt. But God used her courageous decision to change my life in profound ways.

The Emotionally Healthy Woman is based on Geri's story, but it could equally have been titled, *The Emotionally Healthy Man*. Every person who follows Jesus needs to discover and apply these truths that have become so disconnected from our spiritual formation in Christ. I recommend this book as indispensable reading to every male pastor and church member to whon I speak around the world.

Until now, I have been the chief beneficiary of this message, learning up close from Geri each of the "Quits" described in this book. Over the last seventeen years I have learned *how to* quit as a parent, a husband, and a pastor/leader. While initially difficult, this journey has led to a level of freedom and joy in the Christian life that I never imagined was possible.

In fact, the eight "Quits" described here are foundational to our spiritual formation ministries and leadership values at New Life Fellowship Church in Queens, New York. Without courageous women and men who will take up the challenge of this book, I remain doubtful about our ability to raise up healthy, biblical communities that effectively engage the world with the gospel and deeply transform lives. For this reason I am so excited that the richness and breath of this message is now available to a larger audience through this book.

I love Geri. And she is far from perfect. Nonetheless, after twenty-eight years of marriage, I can gladly affirm that she is my number-one hero. Her life is her greatest gift.

PETER SCAZZERO
Senior Pastor, New Life
Fellowship Church
Queens, New York City

When You Can't
Take It Anymore

The Emotionally Healthy Woman is a book about following Jesus and summoning the courage to quit anything that does not belong to his kingdom or fall under his rule. This is not all you need to grow into a spiritually/emotionally mature adult, but one thing is sure: you cannot get there without it.

Traditionally, the Christian community hasn't placed much value on quitting. In fact, just the opposite is true; it is endurance and perseverance we most esteem. For many of us, the notion of quitting is completely foreign. When I was growing up, quitters were considered weak, bad sports, and babies. I never quit any of the groups or teams I was part of. I do remember briefly quitting the Girl Scouts, but I soon rejoined. Quitting is not a quality we admire—in ourselves or in others.

> The kind of quitting I'm talking about isn't about weakness or giving up in despair.

The kind of quitting I'm talking about isn't about

weakness or giving up in despair. It is about strength and choosing to live in the truth. This requires the death of illusions. It means ceasing to pretend that everything is fine when it is not. Perpetuating illusions is a universal problem in marriages, families, friendships, and work places. Tragically, pretending everything is fine when it's not also happens at church, the very place where truth and love are meant to shine most brightly.

Biblical *quitting* goes hand in hand with *choosing*. When we quit those things that are damaging to our souls or the souls of others, we are freed up to choose other ways of being and relating that are rooted in love and lead to life. For example ...

When we *quit* fear of what others think, we *choose* freedom.

When we *quit* lies, we *choose* truth.

When we *quit* blaming, we *choose* to take responsibility.

When we *quit* faulty thinking, we *choose* to live in reality.

Quitting is a way of putting off what Scripture calls falsehood and the old self. As the apostle Paul writes, "You were taught ... to put off your old self ... and to put on the new self, created to be like God in true righteousness and holiness. Therefore each of you must put off falsehood and speak truthfully to your neighbor" (Ephesians 4:22–25).

When we quit for the right reasons, we are changed. Something breaks inside of us when we finally say, "No more." The Holy Spirit births a new resolve within us. We rise above our fears and defensiveness. The hard soil of our heart becomes soft and ready to receive new growth and possibilities.

The Bible teaches that there is a time and season for everything under heaven (Ecclesiastes 3:1). That includes quitting. But it must be done for the right reasons, at the right time, and in the right way. That's what this book is about.

Cutting the Rope

In 1985, Simon Yates and his climbing partner, Joe Simpson, had just reached the top of a 21,000-foot peak in Peru when disaster struck. Simpson fell and shattered his leg. As the sky grew dark and a blizzard raged, Yates tried to lower his injured friend to safety. At a certain point, however, he accidentally lowered Simpson over an ice cliff, where he hung helplessly. Straining to hold his partner's body in midair, Yates was faced with choosing life or death for his friend.

When he could hang on no longer, Yates had to make a hellish decision: cut the rope and save his own life, sending his partner plummeting down to certain death, or face certain death trying to save him.

Yates later related those painful moments, "There was nothing I could do. I was just there. This went on for an hour and a half. My position was getting desperate ... I was literally going down the mountain in little jerky stages on this soft sugary snow that collapsed beneath me. Then I remembered I had a penknife. I made the decision pretty quickly really. To me it just seemed like the right thing to do under the circumstances. There was no way I could maintain where I was. Sooner or later I was going to be pulled off the mountain. I pulled the penknife out."

Yates cut the rope moments before he would have been pulled to his own death.

Certain that his partner was dead, Yates returned to base camp, consumed with grief and guilt over cutting the rope. Miraculously, however, Simpson survived the fall, crawled over the cliffs and canyons, and reached base camp only hours before Yates had planned to leave. In describing his decision to cut the rope, Yates articulates the core inner struggle for each of us to find the resolve to quit well.

> I had never felt so wretchedly alone ... If I hadn't cut the rope, I would certainly have died. No one cuts the rope! It could never have been that bad! Why didn't you do this or try that? I could hear the questions, and see the doubts in the eyes of those who accepted my story. It was bizarre and it was cruel ... However many times I persuaded myself that I had no choice but to cut the rope, a nagging thought said otherwise. It seemed like a blasphemy to have done such a thing. It went against every instinct: even against self-preservation. I could listen to no rational arguments against the feelings of guilt and cowardice ... I resigned myself to punishment. It seemed right to be punished; to atone for leaving him dead as if simply surviving had been a crime in itself.[1]

Quitting can feel like we are severing a lifeline, that someone, possibly even ourselves, is going to die. For this reason quitting is unthinkable to many, especially in the church. It appears "bizarre" and "cruel." Who wants to be unpopular and rock the boat or disrupt things? I sure didn't.

But there comes a point when we cross a threshold and we can't take it anymore. Like Yates, we know we will die spiritually, emotionally, or otherwise unless we quit and choose to do something differently. We finally step over our fears into the great unknown territory that lies before us.

Yates was criticized by some in the mountain-climbing community for violating a sacred rule of never abandoning one's partner—even if both died in the process. Joe Simpson himself passionately defended Yates' choice. Ultimately, Yates's decision to cut the rope saved both their lives.

The "Unfree" Christian

When I fell in love with Christ, I fell hard. As a nineteen-year-old college student, the enormity of God's love overwhelmed me. I immediately began a passionate quest to know this living Jesus, and I was willing to do whatever it took to please him.

I eagerly structured my life around key spiritual disciplines such as reading and memorizing Scripture, prayer, fellowship, worship, fasting, giving financially, serving, silence and solitude, and sharing my faith with others. In my pursuit of Christlikeness, I absorbed books about the importance of spiritual disciplines by such authors as Richard Foster, J. I. Packer, and John Stott. They were helpful in broadening my understanding of Christianity and inspiring me to keep Christ at the center of my life. However, I failed to grasp the truth that a healthy spiritual life includes a careful balance between serving other people's needs and desires and valuing my own needs and desires. Instead, I put most of my efforts into caring for others at the expense of my own soul.

The accumulated pain and resentment of this imbalance led to my first big "quit" at age thirty-seven. After seventeen years of being a committed Christian, I came to realize that excessive self-denial had led me to a joyless, guilt-ridden existence. Jesus invited me into the Christian life to enjoy a rich banquet at his table. Instead, it often felt like I was a galley slave, laboring to serve everyone else at the feast rather than enjoying it myself. In my relationship with Jesus, I'd gone from the great joy of feeling overwhelmed by his love to bitter resentment at feeling overwhelmed by his demands.

Jesus invited me into the Christian life to enjoy a rich banquet ... it often felt like I was a galley slave.

My identity had been swallowed up in putting others before myself. I constantly thought of the needs of our four small daughters. I worried about Pete's responsibilities. I filled in wherever needed to help our growing church. These are all potentially good things, but my love had become a "have to," a "should" rather than a gift freely given. I mistakenly believed I didn't have a choice.

A renewed understanding of my own dignity and human limits enabled me to place loving boundaries around myself. I soon realized this was central to offering a sincere and genuine gift of love to others. Like God's love to us, it must be free. And the extent to which I valued and loved myself was the extent to which I was capable of loving others well.

Dying to Live

Quitting is about dying to the things that are not of God. Make no mistake, it is one of the hardest things we do for Christ. But the good news is that quitting itself isn't just an end; it is also a beginning. Biblical quitting is God's path for new things to come forth in our lives, for resurrection. And yet, the path that leads to resurrection is never easy.

Internal voices alarm us with fears of quitting.

- "What will people think?"
- "I'm being selfish and not Christlike."
- "I will mess everything up."
- "People will get hurt."
- "Everything will fall apart around me."
- "I will jeopardize my marriage."

Everything inside us resists the pain associated with dying—the nonnegotiable prerequisite for resurrection. As a result, we often cave in to our fears as a short-term anxiety-relief strategy. Sadly, this usually leads to painful long-term consequences—ongoing inner turmoil, joylessness, and festering resentments. As a result, we become stuck and ineffective in bearing genuine fruit for Christ. In my case, it resulted in a shrinking heart that sought to avoid people rather than love them.

Yet, it is only through dying that we can truly live. In the words of Jesus, "whoever wants to save their life will lose it, but whoever loses their life for me and for the gospel will save it" (Mark 8:35). And that was what happened when I quit—I got my life back. And what followed were even more transformations that not only changed me but also brought new life to Pete, our marriage, our children, our church, and to countless others.

Quitting has purified my heart. It has demanded I admit truths about myself that I preferred to bury and avoid. Facing flaws and shortcomings in my character, my marriage, my parenting, and my relationships has been scary. At times, I felt like I was cutting the rope that kept me safely tethered to the side of a mountain. But God has used each freefall to purge my heart and to give me a more intimate experience of his mercy and grace. Thus, along with a deeper awareness of my sinfulness, I have become increasingly captured by God's passionate and undeterred love for me.

> Quitting has demanded I admit truths about myself that I preferred to bury and avoid.

Quitting has led me to a dream-come-true marriage with Pete. Over time, as we began to eliminate unhealthy ways of relating and to practice new emotionally healthy skills, our marriage has become a sign and experience of Christ's love for his bride, the church. And quitting impacted the rest of our relationships as well, including our relationship with our children, our extended families, and the larger community of New Life Fellowship Church.

Quitting has taught me to be loyal to the right things. Although "I quit" might sound like it's only about leaving something, I actually gained a renewed commitment to persevere for the right things. I learned how to serve others sincerely rather than begrudgingly. The apostle Paul offers this vivid description of the paradox of quitting:

What happens when we live God's way [*when we quit*]? He brings gifts into our lives, much the same way that fruit appears in an orchard—things like affection for others, exuberance about life, serenity. *We develop a willingness to stick with things*, a sense of compassion in the heart, and a conviction that a basic holiness permeates things and people. *We find ourselves involved in loyal commitments, not needing to force our way in life, able to marshal and direct our energies wisely.* (Galatians 5:22–23 MSG, emphasis added)

I never dreamed quitting would lead to this kind of freedom and fruit. I used to try to produce, through my own efforts, the fruit of the Holy Spirit. But I found out that when we do life God's way, fruit simply appears in the orchard. It is a marvel to behold. I wouldn't trade it for anything in the world.

What I ultimately discovered when I quit was a path into the true purpose of my life—to be transformed by the love of God and, by the Holy Spirit, to slowly become that love for others.

The pages that follow explore eight specific "Quits." While they do build on one another and are meant to be read in order, each chapter also stands alone. You may wish to begin with a chapter that speaks most urgently to your present circumstance. Once you've read that chapter, I encourage you to return to the beginning and read how that content fits into the larger whole.

We don't make the decision to quit just once; each

"Quit" is a lifelong journey. One never really finishes with any of them. I wrote *The Emotionally Healthy Woman* to prepare you to walk through this new journey for the rest of your life.

As you continue your journey of quitting, know that you don't have to figure out everything by yourself. I encourage you to do two things as you read this book. First, gather with a small group to go through *The Emotionally Healthy Woman*. This will provide opportunity for you to talk about and practically apply this material. Secondly, find and rely on wise, experienced mentors to guide you through the complexities of quitting well. Knowing when and when not to quit are equally important!

Let us now begin to explore the first "Quit" — quit being afraid of what others think.

1

Quit Being Afraid of What Others Think

"I quit!" I told my husband. "I'm leaving our church. This church no longer brings me life. It brings me death. I am going to another church."

I had been imagining this very moment for months. Since my husband was the senior pastor of our church, this was no small decision. For years, I made feeble attempts to get him to pay attention, to see my tiredness and frustrations. Finally, I was finished.

"You can't do that!" Pete replied, visibly upset. "That's ridiculous."

I remained silent, determined not to cave in to his anger.

"What about the kids? Where are they going to go? It's impractical! Listen, just one more year and things will smooth out."

I could see his anxiety rising as he came up with more and more reasons why my quitting was a bad idea.

"What about God? Didn't he call both of us to this?

Look at all the good things he is doing. People's lives are being changed!"

Who could argue with that? Pete had been pulling out the God card since the beginning of our marriage.

For years, I'd felt brushed off and ignored by Pete, and I didn't care anymore. I had finally hit bottom. With Pete pouring so much of his life into the church, I felt like a single parent raising our four young girls alone.

Only a few months earlier, I had told Pete, "You know, if we separated, my life would be easier because then you would at least have to take the kids on the weekends and I would get a break." I meant it, but it was still only a fantasy, an empty threat. My need to be what other people wanted and expected me to be was far too great to actually allow me to stand up for myself.

While I had been a committed Christian for many years, my primary identity was defined not by God's love for me but by what others thought of me. This negatively impacted every area of my life—marriage, parenting, friendships, leadership, even my hopes and dreams.

But now I had lost the fear of what others might think or say. There was no longer anything else left to lose. I had given so much of myself away that I no longer recognized myself. Gone was the creative, outgoing, fun, assertive Geri. Now I was sullen, depressed, tired, and angry.

Our church was growing and exciting things were happening in people's lives, but it came at a too-high cost—a cost I no longer wanted to pay. There was something desperately wrong with winning the whole world for Christ at the cost of losing my own soul.

I complained to Pete about my unhappiness and blamed

him for my misery. To make matters worse, I felt ashamed and guilty about it all. After all, weren't good pastors' wives supposed to be cooperative and content? Still, I got to the point where I was so miserable that I didn't care what *anybody* thought of me. I no longer cared if people saw me as a "bad pastor's wife" or a "bad Christian."

I wanted out.

It has been said that a person who has nothing left to lose becomes the most powerful person on earth. I was now that person.

I started attending another church the next week.

As I look back, I am deeply sad and embarrassed it took me so long to finally take action. The fear of what others might think paralyzed me for years.

Quitting the church was only the first small step toward true freedom in Christ. The problem, I would learn, was not ulti-mately the church, Pete, the congestion of New York City, or our four young children. The hard truth was that the primary problem was me. Monumental things *inside* of me needed to change.

> *The hard truth was that the primary problem was me. Monumental things inside of me needed to change.*

Looking to Others to Tell Me "I'm Okay"

Unwittingly, Pete and I had become like emotional Siamese twins. We were joined at the hip in an unhealthy way. I wanted Pete to think and feel as I did; Pete wanted me to think and feel as he did. He thought I should feel the anguish and passion he did for planting a church in

New York City. I thought he should feel my distress at the difficulties in our lives—long hours, little money, no breaks, difficult people.

We were also joined at the hip in feeling responsible for each other's sadness, anger, and anxiety. As a result, we lived in reaction to one another—minimizing, blaming, denying, and defending ourselves against each other's emotions. Radical surgery was required to separate our emotional worlds. We weren't separate enough as individuals to enjoy genuine connection and togetherness. I feared the negative consequences if I changed our emotional dance. While Pete was not an ogre by any means, I still feared his disapproval because it went right to the core of my identity: if Pete was mad at me, then I felt I must be bad. The very thought of Pete, or anyone for that matter, thinking poorly of me felt worse than death.

But one thing was clear: I was already dying. I couldn't breathe.

For the first nine years of our marriage, I conformed and accommodated myself to Pete's desires. I quickly dismissed my desire to go back to school because it clashed with Pete's already overloaded schedule. I avoided "hot button" topics I suspected might arouse tension in our marriage. I was unable to tolerate the discomfort and pain of Pete's pouting or, worse yet, his anger toward me. What was I to do? Wouldn't he be miserable if I started to be my own person?

Yet, I soon realized this issue went much deeper and wider than my relationship with Pete. Unhealthy patterns of self-sacrifice and accommodation overflowed into every area of my life—in friendships, church, parenting, and my family of origin.

Like most people, I enjoy it when people tell me, either verbally or nonverbally, that I am okay. This is a good thing. I enjoy being supported and accepted by Pete and others. The problem comes when validation from others becomes something one *must* have. Sadly, I needed it; I *had* to have it in order to feel good about myself. In other words, I was okay with myself as long as I felt others were okay with me.

Our "Okayness"

Relying on the approval of others for our sense of self-worth is a direct contradiction of biblical truth. Our "okayness" —that is, our lovability, our sense of being good enough— ultimately must come not from others but from two foundational realities:

We are made in God's image. Being made in God's image means we have inherent worth. We are sacred treasures, infinitely valuable as human beings apart from anything we do.

We have a new identity in Christ. When we begin a relationship with Christ, we find our new identity in him. We now rely on Jesus' sinless record for our relationship with God. We are lovable, "okay," and good enough because of Christ. There is nothing left to prove.

For years, I memorized key verses, did Bible studies on Galatians and Romans, and meditated on the righteousness of Christ as the foundation of who I am. Nonetheless, large portions of my identity remained untouched by the truth of Christ's love for me. My daily reality was that my lovability came not from Christ but from how others perceived me. I needed people to think I was a great Christian and a good person. As a result, I often found myself saying yes when I wanted to say no even when I was miserable.

Large portions of my identity remained untouched by the truth of Christ's love for me.

I relate to the apostle Peter in his struggle to become free from what others think. After Jesus' arrest, the twelve disciples desert him and flee. Peter, however, follows him into an outside courtyard during Jesus' trial and is recognized by various people as his friend. Yet he denies knowing him three times. His fear of disapproval overrides what he knows and believes intellectually to be true. Peter previously confessed Jesus as the Messiah, yet this conviction is not deep enough *in* him to stand up to people's possible rejection and disapproval (Matthew 26:31–75).

In the same way, my identity in Jesus was not as anchored as I imagined. Although my marriage and church were significant sources of pain for years, I was fearful of tampering with these systems. Like the apostle Peter, I could not stand up to rejection and disapproval. I finally acknowledged that my biggest obstacle in making healthy changes was fear of what others might think of me.

That shocking truth rocked me to the core. Like Peter, I was living an illusion. I believed in Jesus as Lord and as the Christ. I enjoyed the love of God to a certain level, but it didn't penetrate deeply enough to free me from being afraid of what others thought.

Biblical Heroes Wandering Off Track

You and I are not alone in this approval addiction. Scripture is filled with examples of people who got sidetracked by looking to others to tell them they were okay.

Abraham, for example, lied out of fear for his own safety—a fear of what the Egyptian king might do if he found out Sarah was Abraham's wife (Genesis 12:10–20; 20:1–18).

Jacob lived out of fear of what other people thought. He went along with his mother's lies rather than confronting her (Genesis 27).

Reuben preferred to treat his brother Joseph kindly rather than sell him out as a slave, but the pressure of nine brothers overwhelmed him. Concerned about what they would think if he were the only defender of his younger brother Joseph, he joined with them in a dreadful crime (Genesis 37:12–36).

Aaron went along with the discontented congregation waiting for Moses to come down from Mount Sinai after forty days. The people wanted a god they could see and touch, so Aaron finally succumbed to the pressure and built a golden calf to ease their anxiety (Exodus 32).

Timothy's tendency to be fearful and give in to those around him almost caused the church in Ephesus to be taken over by false teachers (1 Timothy 1).

In all of these situations, the consequences of looking to others rather than God for validation and approval were disastrous—for the people themselves, for their relationship with God, and for the people they loved. So it is with us.

Wandering Off Track Today

We say Christ has changed our lives. But has he really? How deeply? Consider a couple of present-day scenarios.

You go out to lunch with six other people. You are strapped financially but go because you really enjoy these people and you want to spend time with them. You order salad and water at a cost of six dollars to stay within your budget. Meanwhile, everyone else orders entrees, appetizers, drinks, and desserts. You become nervous when you realize the waitress has put the entire order on one bill. You silently pray they will not divide the bill equally.

"They would never do such an insensitive thing," you repeatedly mutter to yourself.

After a two-hour time of sharing and eating, someone enthusiastically recommends, "What if we make things easy by just dividing the bill equally? It averages to about twenty-five dollars each, including the tip."

"Yes, that's great," everyone chants in agreement.

"Twenty-five dollars each!" you angrily think to yourself. "I don't want to spend that kind of money, but what can I do?"

On the inside, you're dying, but you say nothing because you don't want to ruin the festive atmosphere or, worse yet, be seen as cheap. You pay the twenty-five dollars but feel resentful and vow that you'll never do this again. A month later, you lie when refusing a lunch invitation from the same group by telling them you have a previous commitment.

Here's another example.

Joyce is a longtime Bible study leader and a model for

many in her church. Joyce tries out a new hair stylist recommended by a good friend. However, as she sits in the chair, she grows uneasy about what she is seeing in the mirror.

Inside, she is thinking, "Oh, no! I don't like this haircut at all! This is a disaster." Despite her growing alarm, she says nothing to the stylist. She continues to smile on the outside and make small talk, all the while praying the torture will end soon and that the damage will be manageable.

When the beautician finally finishes, Joyce can scarcely contain her anger. Nevertheless, she thanks the stylist profusely in front of the other customers. In fact, she feels so guilty about her anger toward the woman that she tips her *double*!

Sometimes our need for others to tell us we are okay is so subtle and pervasive it can be both difficult and frightening to recognize it in ourselves. Let's consider a few more scenarios.

- You are hurt by a friend's comment, but you say nothing because you don't want to be thought of as touchy or irritable.
- Your mechanic gives you a bill almost double what he originally quoted to repair your car, but he is busy with other customers, and you don't want to make a scene by asking for an explanation.
- You are out with a group of friends who want to see a movie. Everyone except you wants to go see a particular movie, but you don't want to be seen as difficult or disagreeable, so you go along and don't say anything.

- Your family wants you to attend your aunt's retirement party sixty miles away. You do not want to attend, but you go anyway rather than face your family's disapproval.
- You remain in an unhealthy dating relationship with someone because you don't know how to end it. You're afraid of the repercussions with mutual friends and wonder if people will think, "What is wrong with him? Another failed relationship? Does she want to be single forever?"
- You are visiting with neighbors but don't discipline your four-year-old child's misbehavior because you fear he or she might embarrass you with another temper tantrum.
- You have an employee who is underperforming and being a drag on the rest of the team. You keep hinting about the need for change, but he is not getting the message. You are the supervisor but cannot bear the thought of causing him to lose his job. Rather than fire him, you hire another person to cover for him. Your resentment grows.
- Your boss uses inappropriate language around you, some of which is sexual in nature. You say nothing lest he think you are a "stuck-up prude."
- You haven't changed your hairstyle for more than ten years because your spouse is so against it. Yet you resent how much time you spend to take care of it and long for a change.
- You would like to speak to your spouse about your sex life but are afraid to say anything. You are not sure how he might react.

Pay attention to yourself over the next few days.

Observe your interactions with others. Determine the number of times your words and actions change in order to gain the approval, or avoid the disapproval, of others. The shifts we make in our behavior are often subtle and beneath the level of our consciousness. So be alert!

Loving Yourself for God's Sake

For many Christians today, the love of God in Christ remains an intellectual belief we affirm rather than an experiential reality that transforms our thoughts and feelings about ourselves. As a result, we continue to look for love from other people in destructive ways. Bernard of Clairvaux, the great Christian leader in the twelfth century, spoke of how the love of God leads to healthy love of self. He called this the four degrees of love.[1]

1. *Loving ourselves for our own sake.* We want to avoid hell and go to heaven, so we do the right things such as attend church, pray, and tithe. When the threat of hell is removed, our spiritual life quickly dissipates.
2. *Loving God for his gifts and blessings.* We are happy with God as long as things are going well in our lives. When trials and setbacks begin, we become disappointed and withdraw from him.
3. *Loving God for himself alone.* At this stage, our love for God is not based on our feelings or our circumstances. We love and trust him for the beauty and goodness of who he is, not for what we can get out of him. We see our setbacks and sufferings as gifts to strengthen our faith and love for him.

4. *Loving ourselves for the sake of God.* At this fourth and highest level, the width, length, height, and depth of Christ's love—a love that surpasses human knowledge—has now penetrated the depth of our being, setting us free from our need to borrow that love from others.

The gospel frees us to understand who we are in the light of God's love for us in Christ Jesus. We have value and significance but not for what we do or what others might say. We are "love worthy" because God loves us. God's perfect love drives out any fears of what others think. We discover that his love, as the psalmist writes, is better than life (Psalm 63:3).

Four Reasons to Stop Living for the Approval of Others

If we don't break through our need for the approval of others, our growth is seriously stunted. We cannot mature into spiritual adulthood. A wall is erected that stands between us and the beautiful future God has for us. We settle for the pseudo-comfort of being okay with ourselves based on others being okay with us.

Few of us enjoy "rocking the boat." We prefer playing it safe. Changing our situations can be frightening and the obstacles may appear insurmountable. These fears range from fear of losing our spouses, our jobs, and our friendships to fears of losing the respect of people whom we love.

When change seems so overwhelming, God frequently

uses pain to open us to his supernatural power. When the rich young ruler walks away from the radical life change Jesus has offered to him, the disciples, frightened that change is impossible, ask, "Who then can be saved?" Jesus replies, "With man this is impossible, but with God all things are possible" (Matthew 19:25–26).

> *If we don't break through our need for the approval of others, our growth is seriously stunted.*

Change is difficult and often disrupts the systems of our marriages, churches, friendships, families, or work places. Jesus models for us that death to the approval of others is necessary in order to experience the fruit of resurrection life, which is his freedom, joy, and love.

Is it any wonder we avoid making the kind of colossal move required for this first quit?

There are four common motivators that typically compel people to finally say, "No more!"[2] As you read through each one, consider whether or not there is a similar situation or relationship in your own life.

1. You Violate Your Own Integrity

You violate your integrity when what you believe is no longer what you live. You ignore values that you hold dearly. A wall exists between what goes on inside of you and what you express to others. Who you are "on stage" before others is not who you are "off stage" when you are by yourself.

For example, at work, you can no longer continue lying to cover for your boss out of fear of losing your job. You finally speak up, ready to lose your job if necessary. Or perhaps your parents want you to pursue a certain career. They sacrificed their dreams so you could attend a particular school. You'd prefer to do something else but can't imagine saying no to them—especially in light of all they have sacrificed for you. You finally realize that something inside of you is dying and that you need to respectfully speak with them about your passions and desires.

We observe this same dynamic in one of the most dramatic episodes of the New Testament. When the apostle Peter first arrived in Antioch from Jerusalem, he welcomed and ate with uncircumcised Gentile Christians. Later a group of professing Jewish Christians arrived from Jerusalem, convincing Peter to withdraw and separate from these Gentiles. They argued that it was against God's will to eat with Gentiles because they were considered unclean. When the apostle Paul observed this, he publicly confronted Peter for his hypocrisy (Galatians 2:11–14).[3] Paul risked being slandered and misunderstood, endangering his position, reputation, and future. If Paul had chosen to be silent, he would have violated his own integrity about the truth of the gospel.

Scripture notes that Peter "was afraid of those who belonged to the circumcision group" from Jerusalem (Galatians 2:12). He feared their disapproval. Where might you see yourself in this story? Are you like Peter, desiring the approval of others and acting in a way inconsistent with your values? Or are you like Paul, with an identity so anchored in Christ's love that you are able to cut through the disapproval of others and do what is good and true?

2. *What or Whom You Love Is at Stake*

You realize that if you continue your present course and behavior, you will lose someone or something dear to you. This may be your spouse, family, career, future, or even yourself. To make a change feels awful, but to stay where you are is even worse.

> To make a change feels awful, but to stay where you are is even worse.

Perhaps your husband has an addiction to pornography. You love him, but it's clear he's not taking steps to get the help he needs. The cost of not doing anything has now become too high. You begin to see that your unwillingness to disturb the peace is costing you the very marriage you so want to save. You finally say, "No more," and find a mature friend or professional counselor to help you identify possible next steps.

John, a member of our church, works inhuman hours. His driven, overbearing boss expects him to work six days a week and be on call on Sundays. The few precious hours he has for his family on Sunday are often interrupted. His salary provides a good income for his family, but his inability to set boundaries with his boss creates a growing resentment in his home. Jane, his wife, struggles with depression and increasingly finds she is unable to parent their four children, ages four to eleven. John sees his wife and family slipping away.

To medicate his inner turmoil, John begins drinking each night after work. After several months, John reaches such a low point that he no longer recognizes himself. At last he concludes, "If I am not willing to risk the loss of my boss's approval, I am going to lose my own soul and my family." So he knows what he must do. John will assert himself to his boss and is ready to face the consequences.

3. *The Pain of Your Present Situation Is So Great You Have to Make a Change*

Some of us have such a huge tolerance for pain that it takes an explosion to get us to move. One attractive, highly educated, young woman I know went in and out of an abusive relationship because she was so familiar with such treatment from her family of origin. The pain eventually led her to leave the relationship completely. As she began to receive Christ's love, her identity was remolded, and she was able to value herself the way Christ does.

Parker Palmer, a well-known educator and writer, describes a crippling depression that stemmed from trying to live a life that was not his own. This agony led him to break free from the tyranny of other people's approval and follow his unique, God-given path.[4] For a friend of ours, it took a doctor telling him that he was one step away from a massive heart attack in order for him to make some long-overdue changes in his stressed-filled life.

Perhaps you've hated your job for several years. The ongoing boredom and lack of challenge of staring at a computer all day are killing you. But you are afraid of launching out to make a change. You wonder if you have any marketable skills or if the economy might experience another downturn. Despite your fear of being jobless, there is no longer a question of staying. "Facing the unknown cannot be worse," you decide, "than my present situation."

4. The Fear That Things Will Stay the Same Is Greater Than the Fear That Things Will Change

The notion of changing our situation can easily overwhelm us. There comes a point, however, when the thought of remaining in certain circumstances another one, five, ten, or thirty years is more terrifying than risking change. At times, this serves as a clear message from God to get off the road you are on. Change becomes less scary than the prospect of remaining where you are.

You are a high school English teacher. You love English, but teaching teenagers is a tug-of-war that you loathe. Seized by fear at the thought of doing this the rest of your life, you leave the security of a paycheck and the career for which you prepared. You pursue other possibilities and experiences to find a better match for your gifts and passions.

You are single and in a long-term relationship that is stuck and going nowhere. As you imagine your life ten years from now, the risk of being alone becomes less frightening than remaining trapped in the same place with this person. The reality shocks you into finally ending the relationship.

You have sixty thousand dollars in credit card debt and fear bankruptcy. Your future choices are limited and bleak. The fear that this debt is going to ruin you finally becomes greater than the fear of dramatically changing your lifestyle. You begin an in-depth budgeting course and radically adjust your spending habits.

This fear was a contributing factor that finally propelled me into changing my situation. The fear that things would never change in our church or our marriage became greater than my fear of quitting the church and risking the displeasure of others. I reached the bottom in terms of what I was willing to put up with. My dread that life could remain like this for the next twenty years moved me to finally say, "No more!"[5]

A Healthy Model

By adulthood we accumulate millions of messages, spoken and unspoken, from our families, cultures, even our churches. They tell us what we must do, be, think, and feel to be loved, accepted, and approved. For this reason, making the decision to quit being afraid of what others think is not a one-time act but an ongoing spiritual discipline. The depth of our twisted desire for a counterfeit validation outside of the love of God is more far-reaching than we realize. Yet Jesus died, rose, and gave us his Spirit so that we might experience ongoing transformation and freedom.

> *The depth of our twisted desire for a counterfeit validation outside of the love of God is far-reaching.*

John 12 tells the story of Mary, who provides a model of what it means to ground our identity in Christ's love for us rather than in what others think. Mary lets down her hair in public and washes Jesus' feet as if she were a lowly Gentile slave. In ancient Jewish culture this was considered scandalous behavior. Is she trying to seduce Jesus? Doesn't she have any self-respect? Is she not aware of what people might say about her?

Sitting at the feet of Jesus, Mary is not preoccupied

with what others think of her. Christ's love and forgiveness penetrate her inmost being. This profound experience not only releases her from any sense of shame; it
illumines the truth about her own worth and value. Her
heart brims over with thankfulness to Jesus for his love,
mercy, and overwhelming safety.

Mary understands her own significance in relation to
Jesus rather than in the opinions of others. Her actions
are not dictated by what is right in the eyes of the world
but by what is right in the eyes of Christ. This gives her
confidence to be herself, regardless of what others might
think about her.

Like Mary, you are invited to ground your identity
in an ongoing experience of the love of God in Christ.
Then, and only then, will you be able to live honestly and
authentically.

Reflect on the Movements of Your Heart and on the Love of God

When it comes to quitting the approval of others, progress
is best made with two daily practices: reflecting on the
movements of your heart and reflecting on the love of
God. For example, to reflect on the movements of your
heart, think back on your recent interactions with people.
What did you say to position yourself so that others would
think well of you? What might you have done differently?
Ask God to help you be aware of the temptation to adjust
your behavior or words for someone's approval.

The second daily practice is to contemplate the love of
God. I spend time regularly in Scripture, in silence and

solitude, receiving the love of God, allowing it to permeate and change every cell in my body. This has proven foundational to slowly dissipate the fear of what others think. The principle is simple: the more you ground your identity in the love of God, the less you need the approval of people for your sense of lovability.

When you are willing to quit caring what others think, you take a giant step into the next "Quit"—quit lying. In the next chapter, we will explore what it means to live in the truth and be set free from lying to ourselves, to God, and to others.

2

Quit Lying

Lying is so much a part of our world—in politics, business, marriage, dating, income tax returns, job applications, advertising, families, friendships, workplaces, school —that we shouldn't be surprised that lying is also pervasive within the Christian community.

- You greet someone with a big smile and a hug, but the truth is you can't stand this person.
- You say, "We're doing just fine in our marriage," when the relationship can best be described as icy and cold.
- You say, "I am doing well. It didn't bother me that I lost my job. I'm not worried," when really you are very afraid for your future.
- You say, "I think you did a great job," when you actually think the performance was adequate at best.
- You say, "Oh, I can't come. I'm too busy," when the truth is you prefer not to attend the event.

Lying and pretense is so deeply ingrained that we rarely notice it. Every culture and every family has their

Lying and pretense is so deeply ingrained that we rarely notice it.

own unique way of spinning half-truths, withholding facts, and avoiding awkward moments. We lie with our words. We lie with our smiles. We lie with our bodies. We lie with our silence. We think nothing of it because "everyone does it."

"Good" Christian Lying

Like most people, I lied before I committed my life to Christ at age nineteen. What is most alarming, though, is how unaware I was of how much lying I continued to do. I lied first and foremost to myself, then to others, even to God.

Looking back, I realized that the churches I attended promoted a variety of unspoken commandments about what was and was not acceptable to say. These commandments encouraged me to pretend things were okay when they were not and to spin truth to keep the peace as a "good Christian."

When I felt emotions such as anger, sadness, or disappointment, I tried to ignore them. Wasn't the Christian life supposed to be joyful and abundant? I asked God to take these feelings away; he didn't. So I kept lying.

During the early years of my marriage, I lied about how miserable I was with the pace of our lives. I lied about how angry I was about feeling like a single parent. I lied about feelings of resentment toward difficult people in the church. I lied about how deeply sad I was living in New York City and apart from nature, beaches, mountains, hiking trails, and open spaces.

I often lied by saying a kind, loving yes to people when, on the inside, I was angry and saying no. I lied out of fear, not wanting to disappoint people.

I gave car rides to people when I preferred to go directly home. I accepted invitations to social events when I longed to be alone. I told Pete I wouldn't mind if he worked late, when I did mind.

For years I felt guilty for being annoyed or angry.

"Geri, is everything okay?" a good friend asked one day, when a couple sharp remarks about my life leaked out.

I quickly covered my tracks. "There's nothing wrong. Everything is just fine." But my tone of voice, sharp words, and body language betrayed me.

Faith's Baby Dedication

I grew up in a family where births of children, holidays, birthdays, and graduations were considered sacred events. I have six siblings, twenty-three nieces and nephews, and, at present, sixteen great-nieces and -nephews. Gathering together at these events is our tradition. We are an Irish-American clan, fiercely loyal and committed. So when Faith, our third daughter was born, we naturally planned a family celebration around her baby dedication.

"Pete, about twenty people from my family are coming in three weeks," I said, hoping he would take time off from church to help with the planning.

"Sure, that's great," he replied as he walked away.

I knew what that meant. The church was in full swing, and he was overwhelmed; I was on my own.

As the day approached, I grew increasingly tense and short-tempered. Taking care of three small children — ages six, four, and now three months — was draining and difficult enough. On top of that, I had sole responsibility for all the preparations needed for the arrival of my family, Pete's family, and our friends.

"I hate how consumed Pete is with the church," I mumbled to myself. At the same time, I felt guilty and selfish. Wasn't he giving himself to all these people out of obedience to Christ? Still, I wanted time with him; I wanted the kids to have time with him — I wanted a break! How do you compete with unselfishness for God, even if it is misdirected?

Three days before the big event, Pete asked if I would figure out babysitting arrangements for our three girls so we could go out on a romantic date.

"You have got to be kidding!" I answered sarcastically. "Why don't you clean the house, do the laundry, send directions to everyone coming from out of town, figure out where people are going to park their cars, and cook for forty people? Oh yes, while you are at it, find the babysitter, too."

He was silent.

There was no romantic date.

Three days later, on a bright April Sunday, my extended family made the arduous trip through the maze of tunnels, bridges, and traffic to visit us in Queens. They came to church that Sunday and then to our tiny, second-floor apartment for the celebration party that began about 1:00 p.m.

Pete was supposed to be home by 2:00 p.m. Of course,

he didn't think about getting someone else to preach for him so he could be at home for the start of our daughter's party, and I didn't ask him to.

"Why should I have to state the obvious?" I thought to myself. But I accepted that he would arrive an hour late when the party was in full swing.

2:00 p.m.—No Pete.

3:00 p.m.—No Pete!

4:00 p.m.—No Pete!! "Where is he? I can't believe this!?"

We were celebrating the birth of our daughter, and I was entertaining his family, my family, and our friends—alone. I felt humiliated.

Our families began to say their good-byes at about 5:15 p.m. As my parents walked out, Pete strolled casually through the door.

"Oh, you're leaving already!" he exclaimed with a look of surprise. "The night is young! I just got caught up in some serious stuff at church."

I was embarrassed in front of my family. What must they be thinking?

"Who cares about some serious stuff at church? This is your daughter!" I shouted inside my head, though I said nothing.

As our family and friends left, Pete frantically tried to clean up the house as an act of penance.

I didn't speak with him the rest of the evening and very little over the next two days. My body language and demeanor were clear: "Stay away. I will let you know when I want to talk to you again."

I assumed Pete knew how difficult this was for me,

how important this event was to me, that we could never get this day back again.

Ever.

For three days, we did not talk about it. When I finally did tell Pete how disappointed I was, I held back about the depth of my anger. How might he react?

Toward the end of our discussion, he acknowledged that his lateness was an indirect way of punishing me for refusing to go on a romantic date with him three days earlier. He confessed this was his way to retaliate for my condescending attitude.

Pete apologized. I extended pardon, as any "good Christian" should, and moved on.

But I lied.

It took another five years for me to tell him the truth of how deeply I was hurt by his actions and that this wound remained open and unhealed.

Degree of Truth, Degree of Freedom

Part of God's beautiful plan, from the beginning, has been for human beings to live in truth. This remains central to his design for our freedom and joy. Jesus said, "If you hold to my teaching, you are really my disciples. Then you will know the truth, and the truth will set you free" (John 8:31–32). This truth includes both biblical truth about God and truth in general.

As followers of Jesus Christ, the degree to which we live in truth is the degree to which we are free. When we lie in certain areas of our life, we shackle and chain ourselves, restricting the freedom Christ won for us.

When a pastor teaches the Bible to his church, then goes home and secretly spends time viewing pornography on the Internet, he is not free but in chains.

The head of the stewardship committee repeatedly exhorts people to give generously, giving the appearance she is leading the way in this effort but hasn't given a penny herself. She fears being found out. She is not free but in chains.

Larry and Tracy present themselves to their small group as a strong, Christian marital couple. Tracy, however, often explodes in anger at Larry. Larry is afraid to talk to Tracy or disagree with her lest things worsen between them. They don't want to admit this problem to themselves or anyone else. Both Larry and Tracy are not free but in chains.

> The degree to which we live in truth is the degree to which we are free.

A great spiritual warfare rages around this issue in our lives. For this reason, Paul cites the belt of truth as the first element of the armor of God that we are to wear to defend ourselves against the powers of evil (Ephesians 6:12–14).

At age thirty-seven, I had been a serious follower of Christ for almost twenty years before I finally discovered what it meant to live in truth and experience freedom in my innermost being (Psalm 51:6). When I quit lying, I decided I could no longer pretend or participate in the crazy façade I understood as the Christian community and church. I could no longer continue to call truth lies and lies truth. The cost of lying had become too great. I finally arrived at the threshold where I had nothing left to lose by being painfully honest with myself, with others, and with God.

Since God is ultimate truth, I unwittingly exclude him from my life whenever I fail to live in truth. When we lie, we are no longer in God's domain but Satan's. Jesus refers to the evil one as the "father of lies" (John 8:44). And once we cross that line, we are vulnerable to a variety of attacks and deceptions. As long as I was dishonest with myself and Pete regarding my true feelings about missing Faith's baby dedication party, the wound remained open.

When I quit lying, I decided I could no longer participate in the crazy façade I understood as the Christian community.

This resulted in my own inner turmoil and lingering resentment toward Pete.

Lying to Self

The person I lied to the most was myself. My desire to look good to others was so deeply ingrained that I continually deceived myself. "Geri, you're not unhappy. You can do this. You can be joyful as God commands."

The problem was that I had grown increasingly miserable and exhausted during the early years of our married life. As young parents with four small children, we started a church in New York City from scratch, without people, staff, or money. Our faith was a mixture of loving God, good and bad theology and training, youthful naiveté, and ignorance of our personal issues. Keeping my soul alive in the midst of such an environment required a lot of lying and denying.

But lying on the inside made it impossible for me to genuinely love others. My inner conflicts combined with repressed sadness and anger rendered me unpredictable and unsafe. Anger smoldered beneath my loving Christian demeanor.

The day I admitted I wasn't really a very loving person was the day I took a huge step toward becoming a loving person. A huge burden of pretense fell from my shoulders, and I could finally admit my real weakness and broken-ness. I was humbled. Embracing my own flaws was what eventually enabled me to become a safer, softer, and more approachable person.

Virginia Satir, a renowned family therapist, has observed that messages or rules we internalize from our families and culture often make it easy to lie to ourselves. Some of these rules are verbalized, though most are not. She writes, "Most of us live inhuman lives because we live inhuman rules about ourselves."[1] As you read some examples of Satir's "inhuman rules," consider if any of these may be unspoken rules that have impacted your life.

- Don't show your feelings.
- Don't show off.
- Don't talk back.
- Always be nice.
- Don't fight.
- Always be good.
- Obey authority at all times.
- Always be on time.
- Don't boast; pride goes before a fall.
- Mistakes can kill, so never make one.

"Most of us live inhuman lives because we live inhuman rules about ourselves."
Virginia Satir

When these rules are unconsciously carried into adult-hood and never challenged, they smother our freedom and encourage lying. I tell myself, for example, that I'm not angry because I have a rule that I'm always supposed to be nice. I tell myself that I'm not disappointed because I have a rule that says, "I need to be good and good people aren't sad or disappointed." I say yes to people when I mean no because I have a rule that says, "Nice people always say yes."

When we grow up with family rules like these, we easily can end up lying to ourselves about our needs and desires. We tragically restrict important aspects of who God made us to be. Inevitably, we limit our God-given freedom to choose and minimize the God-given truth about who we really are.

Lying to Others

A study published by Robert Feldman, a psychologist at the University of Massachusetts, found that lying is closely tied to self-esteem. It concluded that the more people feel their self-esteem is threatened, the more they lie. In the study, people became increasingly engaged in managing how others perceived them and, as a result, said more and said things that were not entirely accurate. Feldman concluded, "We're trying not so much to impress other people but to maintain a view of ourselves that is consistent with the way they would like us to be."[2]

For this reason it is often easier to lie to others — to skim on the truth — than to risk saying what's true. It seems easier to say nothing after being hurt by a coworker's insensitivity than to confront him or her. It seems easier to say yes to a dinner meeting with the boss than to admit we have a family commitment. It seems easier to spin a few facts to a client rather than possibly lose a contract. It seems easier to give the impression I am a strong and growing Christian than to acknowledge spiritual stagnation.

Why? Few of us are comfortable looking badly in the eyes of others or ourselves. We forfeit the truth to not only please the person in front of us but also ensure a positive image of ourselves,[3] whether it is true or not. Consider the following scenario as it highlights additional nuances and complexity around lying to others.

Christina comes home from her hair appointment and finds her husband sitting at the kitchen table reading the newspaper with a cup of coffee. She taps him on the shoulder.

"Mike, do you like my haircut?"

He looks up from behind the newspaper. His eyebrows lift slightly. He nonchalantly examines this new curly look on his wife.

"No, not really," he replies, returning his gaze to the paper.

"What?" she yells. "Sometimes I can't believe how insensitive you are!"

Christina is hurt and angry as she retreats to the bathroom to take a closer look at the apparent disaster of her haircut.

In such a situation, what would you recommend to Mike? Why couldn't he simply state, "It looks great, honey"? Wouldn't it be more loving to utter a little lie rather than hurt his wife?

What might it mean for Mike not to lie? Could he state the truth with a little more grace?

Imagine Mike saying to Christina, "I love you, honey, for who you are. What *you* think and feel about your haircut is more important than what I think. But with that said, I have preferred other haircuts."

Lying may provide short-term relief. It comes, however, at a cost.

Or try to visualize Mike answering thoughtfully and honestly, "This haircut is not my favorite, but you are always beautiful to me."

Many different factors need to be taken into account for a respectful, honest, mature response by Mike. For example, how much goodwill exists in their relationship? What is their marital history? What is their personal level of awareness and maturity?

The person, surprisingly, who unconsciously lies in this story is Christina when she poses the question to Mike: "Do you like my haircut?" She is not asking an honest question. What she's really trying to communicate is, "I'm scared and anxious that I may not look good. I want and need you to tell me I'm okay." Christina's question is in itself a lie.

Since Christina does not seem comfortable in herself or in the haircut, she wants Mike to validate her. Because her appearance is important to her—as it is to most of us—even something like a haircut can cause her to wander from resting in the love of Christ. For many of us, just as it is for Christina, lying is rooted in the need for others to validate and affirm us so we feel good about ourselves.

Lying may provide short-term relief. It comes, however, at a cost. What seems like a harmless lie at the moment becomes more complicated and difficult with time. The easy way out turns out to be more difficult. Our relation-ships grow more distant and diminish in quality. People's trust in us lessens. Our stress increases. We carry more anxiety in having to remember what version of reality we told people. And most importantly, our ability to love God and others, the very meaning of our existence, worsens.

Conflict? Something May Be Right!

Author Sandra Wilson has said, "The truth sets us free, but it first makes us miserable."[4] In relationships built on half-truths or untruths, the truth may actually be the beginning of the end. Once we start being truthful, it may make or break some of our relationships.

As I began to be truthful with Pete, we experienced a new level of conflict in our relationship that could no longer be ignored. We had been stuck in our differences, unable to find a way out. Speaking the truth changed all that. Conflict with Pete, although initially difficult and painful, eventually led to the intimate mar-riage for which I had dreamed.

Most of us believe conflict is a sign of something going wrong, but the reverse is often true. It may indicate that everything is going *right*. Conflict is normal, important, and necessary when close relationships enter into a new cycle of growth and maturity.

> *Conflict is a sign of something going wrong, but ... it may indicate that everything is going right.*

Speaking truth does not ensure a wel-comed response from your listener. Truth spoken irrespon-sibly or disrespectfully almost always creates unnecessary damage. Remember, the Lord came full of grace and truth (John 1:17). Speaking the truth in love involves choosing the right timing, using words respectfully, taking responsibility for our own thoughts and feelings, and speaking in the "I." We are not born with these skills; they must be learned and practiced.

The Practice of Speaking the Truth

It is one thing to stop lying; it is quite another to start speaking the truth. Speaking the truth skillfully is one of the most significant ways we acknowledge and respect the image of God in ourselves and others. Learning how to speak the truth is crucial for spiritual maturity. At New Life Fellowship Church we teach people to practice speaking the truth *respectfully, honestly, clearly,* and *timely.*

> ***Respectfully.*** Think before you speak in order to describe carefully what you want to say. Be *polite*, not insulting, taking the other person's feelings into account.
>
> Disrespectful: "That idea stinks …"
>
> Respectful: "That is an interesting idea," or "I'm puzzled by …"
>
> ***Honestly.*** Say what you truly think or feel; don't lie or fudge the truth.
>
> Dishonest: "I can't go to lunch. I have other plans."
>
> Honest: "I prefer not to go to lunch today because I want to have time alone."
>
> ***Clearly.*** Don't beat around the bush or drop hints to avoid truth. Don't make a statement when you are really asking a question. Include details.

Unclear: "There is a good movie playing at the theater, but it's raining out."

Clear: "Would you be willing to go to the movies with me tonight even though it is raining out?"

Unclear: "I'd like you to cook dinner sometimes."

Clear: "I would like you to cook dinner Tuesdays and Thursdays and be responsible for all the ingredients you need."

Timely. Pick a time that will be beneficial to both speaker and listener, when they are not tired, distracted, or tense.

Untimely: Your daughter comes home from a hard day at school with disappointment around her grade on a math test and a conflict with a good friend. You begin to talk about her messy room.

Timely: You realize your daughter is struggling from a hard day at school. You wisely decide to wait for a better time when she is more relaxed to talk with her about her messy room.

This takes thought and energy. Remember, you probably have a lifetime of not speaking respectfully, clearly, or in a timely way. Few of us have observed it modeled in our families and cultures. Give yourself lots of time and grace to practice this new skill.

Lying to God

Many people actually lie to God, only sharing with him what they think he wants to hear or what they *ought* to feel. I was one of them. Consider the absurdity of such a notion, as if God didn't know us better than we know ourselves. After becoming honest with myself, I finally became brutally honest with him.

For years I experienced inner conflict. I was a committed Christian, yet I struggled with thoughts and feelings that I didn't believe were acceptable. Sadness and anger, for example, filled me with guilt and shame. They were flaws to be suppressed and denied. I repeatedly asked God, "Restore to me the joy of your salvation" (Psalm 51:12). Sadly, I did not understand how God could be speaking to me through the pain of my inner world.

In contrast, biblical models of genuine spirituality embrace their inner worlds and don't lie about them. The prophets Elijah and Jonah honestly told God they preferred to die (1 Kings 19:1 – 5; Jonah 4:8). Job prayed wild prayers by cursing the day of his birth after losing his ten children and his health. John the Baptist, in deep inner struggle, honestly expressed to Jesus his confusion about the truth of Jesus being the Messiah. God calls us neither to spin nor to cover up in our relationship with him. We are to face, in God's presence, all our disappointments and struggles (large and small) along with all their accompanying confusing emotions.

I mistakenly thought that if I didn't say certain things out loud, then they weren't a reality, even to God. He wouldn't know how angry, depressed, ashamed, hopeless, or confused I felt—as if he didn't already know all my thoughts and feelings. The more I grew in authenticity with myself, the more I grew in knowing God. Scripture and grace came alive in new ways.

Through a courageous commitment to truth, we go forward, hand in hand with God, experiencing his promise that the truth sets us free.

Ending Pretense for a Taste of Heaven

Make no mistake about it, saying "I quit" to lying and making a commitment to tell the truth will initially feel like death because it is so ingrained in us. However, it is a good death, ultimately leading to life and resurrection.

Once you end the pretense of superficiality and "niceness" that characterizes so much of Christian culture today, you will experience liberation, freedom, and a genuine body life that is truly a taste of the kingdom of heaven. Your relationships grow more authentic. With nothing to hide, your stress levels and anxieties decrease. Your self-esteem grows more solid because your integrity isn't broken. Peace with God, yourself, and others permeates your life.

When you quit lying, you are awakening to the "true self" God has planted within you.

When you quit lying, you ignite your spirituality. You are removing false layers and awakening to the "true self" God has planted within you. By God's grace you will become among the freest people on earth.

And there will be no going back.

Five years after Faith's baby dedication, Pete and I finally had that conversation about my pain and disappointment. Since we had begun practicing truth-telling skills in our relationship, we were able to be respectful, honest, clear, and timely. I wept as I poured out my pain.

He listened. We both knew we could not redo that unique event. We said all we needed to say and we held each other. Pete asked forgiveness. At last, we brought healthy closure to a painful episode in our history.

When we quit lying to ourselves, to others, and to God, a great awakening begins. Parts of us that were previously buried, both good and sinful, now emerge. A new question arises: To what am I to die and to what am I not to die to within myself? Discerning between the good and the sinful is a large subject and leads us to the next chapter —quit dying to the wrong things.

3

Quit Dying
to the Wrong Things

Many Christians live unhappy, unfulfilled lives. Tired, frustrated, and often resentful, they slowly burn out, wondering what went wrong. They are dying to the wrong things. Dying to the wrong things means depriving yourself of God-given gifts and pleasures that nurture your unique life in him.

You die to the wrong things when you set aside or devalue activities that cause your soul to feel fully alive (music, dance, writing, art, astronomy, outdoors); when you ignore important relationships; when you care for others to the detriment of yourself; and when you fail to honestly state your preferences, always deferring to others.

Dying to the wrong things reflects a lack of self-respect and failure to grasp our personal dignity as made in the image of God himself. This can easily lead to a tragic distortion and misapplication of what it means to lay down our lives for Christ.

A Christian or a Nonperson?

During my junior year in college, when I was an exchange student in England, I became a committed follower of Christ. At that point, I had one overriding goal—to love and serve Christ as a response to his sacrificial love for me. I took this statement as my life verse: "Whoever wants to be my disciple must deny themselves and take up their cross and follow me" (Mark 8:34).

After returning to the United States, I became deeply involved in Christian leadership at the university I attended. I led small groups, organized events, and reached out to my network of friends. Pete and I used to joke that we majored in Christ and minored in academics.

After college graduation and teaching high school for two years, I spent three years with InterVarsity Christian Fellowship, serving students at Rutgers University and other colleges in New Jersey. After several years of giving myself fully to students, I was fatigued. But when Pete and I then became engaged, I was filled with hope that our marriage would initiate a new, less-intense chapter in my life.

I had no idea a tsunami was heading my way.

After five months of marriage, I followed Pete's vision to learn Spanish in Central America in order to return to New York City and start a new church. I didn't have my own vision except to be married to Pete. So off to Central America we went to live in an impoverished neighborhood with a family of ten children who spoke no English. Yes, ten children!

After almost a year in Costa Rica, we returned to New

York City. Within our first month home, I gave birth to the first of our four daughters, and Pete immersed himself in teaching and laying the foundation for planting New Life Fellowship Church.

The eight years that followed were a whirlwind of raising small children, hosting streams of new people into our home, rescuing people in crisis, and dealing with the unending demands of starting a new church. I was dying on the inside.

It soon became apparent that a misunderstanding and misapplication of my life verse—"Whoever wants to be my disciple must deny themselves and take up their cross and follow me"—was now killing me. Physically and emotionally weary, I might have been gaining the whole world in terms of productive ministry, but I was also losing my own soul.

The outgoing person I once was disappeared. I grew increasingly depressed and longed to withdraw from people as much as possible. My misery reached such proportions that I did not recognize myself. This is when I quit our church.

Pete and I desperately needed help to sort out the turmoil in our souls, marriage, and church. Under the guidance of a wise counselor, I began to sense life flowing through my veins as I was given permission to express what I really felt and thought. I was affirmed in my anger, hurt, and tiredness.

"Yes, it makes sense you would feel that way," said our counselor. He continued, "Geri, have you ever thought about this principle: The extent to which you love yourself is the extent to which you can love others well." His words poured living water into my dry soul.

A painful truth began to dawn on me: "Maybe I have been denying the wrong parts of myself ... parts that Christ never asked me to die to. Maybe much of our suffering was not for the gospel.[1] Perhaps it was pure stupidity and ignorance!" The very thought was deeply alarming.

Was it possible that I was dying to the wrong things?

A "Good, Loving Christian"?

In my early Christian experience, I learned that a "good and loving Christian" embodied certain qualities. These messages were modeled and encouraged by the Christian subculture in which I was being formed spiritually.

I wanted to be a good, loving Christian no matter the cost. And I mistakenly believed that good, loving Christians were people characterized by five things: they never said no, they had an active social calendar, they juggled many things without complaining, they got things done, and they put others' needs before their own.

They Never Say No

I did not understand the powerful, biblical principle of limits as a gift from the hand of God.[2] God places boundaries around every living thing, including human beings. We are not created to be twenty-four-hour-seven-day-a-week machines. Our bodies and minds need sleep and rest. We have limits specific to our age, personality, marital status, children, gifts, education, family of origin, and economic status.

Yet I assumed that if a need crossed my path, then it was God's will that I should meet it. This was obviously the right thing to do. I felt guilty if I didn't.

My conversations went something like this:

> **Friend:** "Geri, Can you give me a ride home?"
>
> **Geri:** "Sure!"(Even though this will take me way out of my way and I am worn out.)
>
> **Church Member:** "Geri, will you teach this Sunday school class? I was up late last night with my three-year-old and I'm not feeling well."
>
> **Geri:** "Sure!" (Even though I too am exhausted by my own small children.)
>
> **Pete:** "Geri, can we have company for dinner?"
>
> **Geri:** "Sure!" (Even though I prefer to be by ourselves.)

I did not understand the powerful, biblical principle of limits as a gift from the hand of God.

No matter what the request or need, no matter how depleted or empty I felt, I believed that a good and loving Christian would rarely say no.

They Have an Active Social Calendar

My active social life gave me a false sense of goodness and lovability. I mistakenly thought, "I'm a good Christian person if I have a lot of invitations." The more social engagements I attended, the better I felt about myself.

Eventually, these invitations became a terrible burden because I felt compelled to say yes to *all* of them. How many birthday parties, showers, graduations, weddings, luncheons, dinners, and church events can one finite human being attend? Despite my need for solitude, I surrendered my calendar to the social obligations of our church, my large extended family, and our four young girls. It was a recipe for disaster.

They Juggle Many Things without Complaining

I felt this was the real test of my spirituality. Taking another Scripture out of context, I told myself that I can do all things through Christ who gives me strength [cf. Philippians 4:13]—and do them without complaining!

Actually, I ended up complaining a lot, but not clearly or directly. I never admitted, "Our lives are overwhelming, and I don't want to live like this." Instead, I whined and avoided people I was upset with. I typically complained to a third party instead of going to the person directly.

My juggling acts eventually overwhelmed me. I wanted out but felt powerless to do anything about it. I tried to pass my frustration to someone else, usually Pete. Is it any wonder I slipped in and out of depression?

They Get Things Done

Somehow I picked up the belief that the busier I was, the more spiritual and godly I must be. If I was unselfish and sacrificial with my time, then I must be a loving person. The apostle Paul seemed to get a lot done. So did Jesus. So did most of the so-called mature Christian women I

> *Somehow I picked up the belief that the busier I was, the more spiritual I must be.*

knew at the time. I once had a Christian leader tell me he was going to work as much as possible until he died. "I'll have plenty of time to rest in heaven," he remarked. "For now, I'll work as long and as hard as I can."

I did get a lot done. The problem was I was also tired, resentful, and angry.

They Put Others' Needs before Their Own

The guide for my Christian life was summarized in the acronym JOY:

> Jesus first
> Others second
> Yourself third

I had always put others' needs before my own, whether they were my husband's or my children's. I tried, unsuccessfully, to live out my narrow misunderstanding of Paul's command in Philippians 2:3–4: "In humility value others above yourselves, not looking to your own interests but each of you to the interests of the others."

The problem was that it wasn't working. I only grew more miserable as the demands of JOY slowly drained the authentic joy of Christ from my soul.

The Two Tensions

In the early years of my faith, most of my spiritual formation focused primarily on depravity and sin. The good seeds of God hidden beneath my unique person as an image-bearer of God were rarely mentioned. The human heart was considered deceitful *only* and never to be trusted.

Granted, every part of our being is flawed and disfigured by sin. Nonetheless, because of God's image in us, goodness also dwells within every human being. That includes the religiously arrogant, criminals, the homeless, you, and me. Henri Nouwen describes it well:

> For a very long time I considered low self-esteem to be some kind of virtue. I had been warned so often against pride and conceit that I came to consider it a good thing to deprecate myself. But now I realize that the real sin is to deny God's first love for me, to ignore my original goodness. Because without claiming that first love and that original goodness for myself, I lose touch with my true self and embark on the destructive search among the wrong people and in the wrong places for what can only be found in the house of my Father.[3]

An unbalanced biblical theology fails to hold these twin tensions together, resulting in all sorts of confusion about dying to the right and to the wrong things.

Dying to the Wrong Things

As a result of these misguided beliefs, I died to the wrong things. I believed that putting others' needs before my own was what it meant to die to self. In addition to sacrificing myself for the needs of my husband, my children, and the church, dying to self — wrongly understood — also required that I sacrifice myself for the cast of characters who lived on our block.

Across the street from us lived a young, single mother on welfare with six young children. I continually carried the endless burden of helping her out, whether it was driving her to the grocery store, caring for her children, or providing clothes and money.

The drug dealers next door regularly tested my love, patience, and "selflessness." They woke us up many nights as customers honked for their regular drug pickup. Their dogs barked for hours during the day while they slept. They knocked on our front door asking for money. And when screaming fights with their prostitutes broke out late at night, we laid awake hoping it would end quickly.

With these mountains of needs confronting me every day and feeling obligated to say yes to all of them—without complaining—I did experience a kind of dying, but it wasn't dying to self. Instead, I wrongly died to a host of gifts God was inviting me to receive.

I mistakenly died to my delight and love for the outdoors—hiking, lakes, oceans, mountains. I love camping, yet with the intensity of serving Christ and Pete's distaste for camping, I died to my love of nature ... for seventeen years. While we have one lovely tree in our backyard, it is a long way from the great outdoors! As I routinely declined summer vacations at my parents' beach house, my soul shriveled and my resentments grew. Even though I live in urban Queens, God never asked me to die to my love for beauty and the outdoors, even though getting there required a lot of work.

I mistakenly died to my need for silence and solitude. Solo parenting in the early years almost killed me. For years we lived next to a major highway and were forced to endure the sound of speeding cars all night long. With the constant noise and all the people coming in and going out of our home, there was little room for the silence and solitude I longed for.

I mistakenly died to my extended family. I missed significant family events because of church. I missed several women's weekends when my cousins, sisters, and aunts went away together. I missed weddings and other weekend events. I didn't value myself enough to ask Pete to rearrange his life so I could participate in these events. I mistakenly believed I was missing these events because of my commitment to Christ. Like a martyr, I meekly surrendered to my situation.

I mistakenly died to intentional personal growth. I did not develop my leadership gifts or pursue a graduate degree. I took a backseat, a supporting role—not out of a calling from God, but because of gender-based expectations of church culture and my family of origin.

And finally, *Pete and I both mistakenly died* to a great marriage. We did not know what we were missing. It takes time—lots of it—to grow and nurture a mature, intimate, mutually satisfying marriage. We received no training on what it meant to cultivate a great marriage, and there were few, if any, models for us to follow. We simply poured ourselves into loving others at the church and squandered the God-given joys of the first eight years of our marriage.

Have you mistakenly died to anything Christ has not asked you to die to? Pete and I regularly use *The Prayer of Examen* to help us discern if we are dying to the wrong things. We take a few minutes of silence, asking ourselves: "When did I feel most alive this past week? When did I feel the most life draining out of me?"[4]

If we die to the wrong things, ultimately, we end up in disobedience. A Jewish rabbi expressed it well: "For us Jews, studying the Bible is more important than obeying it, because if you don't understand it rightly you will obey it wrongly and your obedience will be disobedience."[5] While he may be overstating to make a point, dying to the right things, and not the wrong things, is essential to a life of faith.

Dying to the Right Things

God never asks us to die to parts of ourselves that bring life to our souls. David, for example, was never asked to give up his love for music and writing poetry. As a busy king under enormous pressure, he could easily have not spent time composing psalms. We benefit, to this day, from his decision to keep writing.

But we are to die to the sinful parts of who we are — defensiveness, arrogance, hypocrisy, a judgmental spirit, finding our worth and value apart from him — as well as the more obvious sins such as gossip, lying, stealing, coveting, and so on. David did have to die to his lying, his concern about what others thought, and his placement of trust in his military power rather than God.[6]

> *God never asks us to die to parts of ourselves that bring life to our souls.*

There is much beneath the surface of our lives that needs excavating if we are to be transformed. Deeply ingrained parts of who we are need to be confronted and put to death. This is the only pathway if we are to walk in the freedom, truth, and love of Christ.

For example, I needed to die to defensiveness and

social shame, to a critical spirit, to the need to be right, to my fears of vulnerability and weakness, and to people's approval. For most of my life, the thought of openly admitting my mistakes and vulnerabilities felt worse than death.

I remember crying on our living room couch with Pete as I wrestled with allowing myself to appear weak before others. It was terrifying, like being a trapeze artist flying high above the ground with no net underneath. Then, in the midst of my terror, I heard God's still, small voice: "Geri, there is a net underneath you. It is the gospel. Christ died for you. You are so loved. You can be weak. You have nothing left to prove."

The illusions about what it meant to be a good, loving Christian crumbled before me. Now I could begin to die to the right things—my self-protectiveness and fears of rejection. It was like being born again, yet again.

Discovering Your Self

Death to self assumes you have a self.

A problem with many Christians begins when we try to sacrifice a self we do not possess. We try to die to our fears, our anger, or our sadness, for example, without first embracing that we are afraid, angry, or sad. We try to die to certain thoughts and feelings that are not of God's kingdom without fully acknowledging they exist within us. We try to love and respect others when we don't love and respect ourselves. We are kind to others when we are not kind to ourselves.

Something that has helped me over the years has been an awareness that "I" exist in two worlds—an external world and an internal world. The external world includes the people to whom I relate and the things going on around me. I experience the external world through my five senses—what I see, taste, touch, smell, and hear. The internal world includes what is going on inside—my thoughts, feelings, values, loves, beliefs, motivations.

> *Death to self assumes you have a self.*

Many people go through life aware mostly of their external, visible world; yet the vast majority of our lives is significantly impacted by the internal world within us. Few of us devote adequate time for the reflection required to cultivate awareness of this interior world.

In my journey in discerning what parts I should die to and what parts I shouldn't, it was crucial to grow in knowing myself. The following three "knowings" helped me uncover the sinful parts that needed to be put to death; they also helped me to reclaim the seeds of my true self that needed to be nurtured. There are three primary areas that you must know and explore if you want to grow in self-knowledge and self-awareness: your heart, your story, and your personality.

Know Your Heart

Knowing your heart means paying attention to the vast array of thoughts and feelings going on inside of you at any given moment. Dag Hammarsjold, former secretary general of the United Nations, describes the challenge before us: "We have become adept at exploring outer space, but we have not developed similar skills in exploring our own personal inner spaces. In fact the longest journey is the journey inward."

Consider the circle below that represents your interior world or your heart.

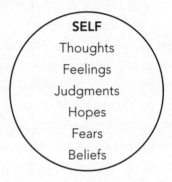

SELF
Thoughts
Feelings
Judgments
Hopes
Fears
Beliefs

The way you think and feel is what makes up your internal self. Your yearnings are you. Your preferences. Your fears. Your beliefs. Your values. Your feelings. Your thoughts. They all reveal you. Before reading any further, consider taking a few minutes or more to journal about what you fear, prefer, value, and so on. This will lead you to uncover more of who you really are in the process. Knowing the depths of our hearts isn't easy; it requires work, often painful work. It calls for openness to the Holy Spirit and time for reflection.

Like many people I meet, my true values — what I considered important — were buried in my subconscious. Because I wasn't sure what my positive values were (things I did like), I started by identifying my negative values (things I did not like). I began journaling in response to this question: What are things I don't like? Here are some of the things I wrote early in my journey.

- I don't like being around angry people.
- I don't like to say "no."

- I don't like crowded places.
- I don't like solo parenting.
- I don't like being married to someone who works constantly.
- I don't like being busy.

Then I asked myself the more difficult questions: What do I value? What is important to me? What are my hopes, my preferences, and my joys? What brings me genuine delight?

As I noted earlier, a number of things to which I had mistakenly died came alive within me — my longing for silence, the outdoors, an intimate marriage, creativity, and exploring new places.

Discerning the values that are important to us takes time.

Failing to acknowledge what is going on in your heart eventually results in losing connection with yourself. And if you lose connection with yourself, you easily slip out of dependency on God's Spirit. Spiritual growth and loving well then become virtually impossible.

Knowing your heart requires standing in God's presence and asking yourself some difficult questions about your actions, reactions, motives, feelings, and thoughts. The following incident illustrates this process.

The neighbor behind our house has a dog who was barking at 11:30 p.m. Lying in bed, I assured myself the barking would end; it didn't.

I drove around the block and knocked on the door.

A middle-aged woman who didn't speak English came to the door. She woke her thirteen-year-old daughter to translate.

"Aren't you aware your dog is barking nonstop in the yard?" I asked in exasperation. "It's nearly midnight! Please bring him in the house."

The daughter then translated for her mother.

"We're afraid of the dog," the young girl responded. The mother nodded her head in agreement.

"What? How can you be afraid of your own dog?" I condescendingly responded.

The Holy Spirit immediately spoke to me. "You were afraid of your dog growing up." That was true.

I didn't say anything to them at that moment. I left. The dog did eventually stop barking. It turns out they called a relative who came over and courageously brought the dog inside.

The next day, as I continued to reflect on the incident, God softened my heart. They weren't stupid for being afraid of their dog—even if it was past midnight. There was nothing else they could do. I was wrong for communicating the way I did and treating them as if they were stupid. I knew what I had to do.

I returned to their house the next day and apologized.

This came about as a result of paying attention to my reaction and being honest about what was really going on in my heart.

God did not ask me to die to the healthy anger that got me out of bed to assert my boundaries. But I had to be honest also about what else was going on in my heart— judgmentalism. My condescending attitude toward them for being afraid of their dog, considering that I had once been afraid of my dog, was the pinnacle of hypocrisy.

When we aren't honest and purposeful about knowing our hearts, we bypass incredible opportunities for transformation.

Know Your Story

In our young and formative years we are like liquid cement into which our families leave deep, unconscious imprints. Those imprints eventually harden and are not easily changed. Only as we grow older do we realize the depth of their influence.

My family gave me many positive legacies for which I am deeply grateful. This included the importance of family, belief in God, and sensitivity to the poor. Unfortunately, I also inherited some negative legacies. For example, I learned unhelpful ways of dealing with conflict and how to avoid unpleasant emotions. These legacies carried over into my adult life and negatively impacted my marriage, my parenting, and my other relationships.

If we say we are in Christ's family but continue to perpetuate unhealthy ways of living learned in our early years, we are fooling ourselves. Things such as sarcasm, defensiveness, perfectionism, retaliation, bitterness, judgmentalism, and unforgiveness do not belong in the family of Jesus. We must look closely at our stories to hold on to that which was good and courageously admit and change that which was not. Only then will we be dying to the right things.

> *If we say we are in Christ's family but continue to perpetuate unhealthy ways of living, we are fooling ourselves.*

In addition to reflecting on the legacies left to us by our families, it is also important to consider other significant people who have shaped us—coaches, mentors, pastors, or teachers. Perhaps a coach repeatedly stressed to a star athlete, "Winning is everything." Now as an adult, she cannot accept setbacks, failures, and disappointments without condemning herself as being a complete failure in every part of her life. We confuse what it means to die and follow Christ when the messages we receive violate the limits of our humanity.

It is also crucial to consider your spiritual history. For example, I have been shaped, both positively and negatively, by my evangelical Christianity. On the positive side, I have learned about the joy of a personal relationship with Christ, the grace of the gospel, love for Scripture, God's heart for the world, and the power of the Holy Spirit. On the negative side, I have learned some things to which I need to die—going beyond my limits, ignoring my weaknesses, avoiding the difficult emotions of anger, sadness, and fear, judging other people's spiritual journeys, and not admitting my brokenness.[7]

When you reflect on your story, what is the life message you received from your mother? Your father? A teacher? Coach? Primary caretaker? Consider, then, what God says about those messages. How does awareness of these things help you know what are the right and the wrong things to die to?

Know Your Personality

Who are you, really? What gives you life? What drains you? What are your defense mechanisms? When do you become self-protective? What tickles your fancy or drives you crazy? Many of us think we know who we are, but we don't. Personality inventories rarely lie and can provide accurate information about ourselves that deepen self-understanding. The insights we receive from these inventories can greatly illuminate what we have to and don't have to die to.

There are seemingly as many personality inventories and tests as there are distinct personalities![8] Whatever test you take or type you identify with, there are two particularly significant factors related to knowing your personality: determining whether you are an introvert or an extrovert and understanding what you are tempted to substitute for God's love in an effort to secure your self-worth.

Are you an introvert or an extrovert? Introversion and extroversion are about what energizes you. Extroverts are energized by the outside world and by being with people; introverts are energized by their interior world and by being alone. I had always thought of myself as a high extrovert since I have strong people skills, enjoy meeting new people, and love being with groups of people. However, I will never forget the first time I took a personality inventory and discovered I was only a moderate extrovert with introvert leanings. I was stunned, but I also felt liberated. It illumined my experiences of fatigue and depression that so often followed unceasing seasons of high-level people activity. This included the preschool years of our four daughters when I did not create space for alone time. I was overjoyed to have my heart's desire—things like solitude and silence—validated and affirmed.

My energy and creativity, I realized, come from an equal amount of being with people and being alone. This gave me the impetus to reorganize my life around larger blocks of alone time, giving my soul the necessary refueling that it needed.

What is the source of your value and self-worth? This refers to how you experience lovability and acceptability, along with what gives you a sense of power. Here are two questions to help you get at the source of your value and self-worth: What do you rely on for significance and meaning? And what core fears motivate your behavior? For me, doing things correctly is extremely important. That is not a bad thing until it becomes a compulsion, or I depend on it instead of on the love of Christ for my value and self-worth. This can lead to an unhealthy perfectionism that hurts the people I love.

While numerous helpful personality tests are available, I believe the Enneagram offers us a more powerful tool as Christ-followers. It identifies the sin tendencies of nine basic personality types, each of which are numbered simply—One, Two, Three, etc. We identify that one major sin or temptation that informs and motivates our behavior and outlook on life. We are then better able to die to the sinful parts of our personality and live out our God-given gifts and uniqueness. With this awareness, we can begin to break free from the sin of putting our values and self-worth in something, or someone, other than God.[9]

What is the source of your value and self-worth?

As you survey the nine Enneagram personality types in the left column of the table on pages 83–87, consider which one best describes you. Then prayerfully reflect on the corresponding remedy in the right column.

Enneagram[10]

The Nine Enneagram Personality Types	What We Must Die To in Order for Christ to Become Our Source of Values and Self-Worth
One. *The Perfectionist (The Need to Be Right).* Ones are motivated by the need to live life the right way, to improve themselves and others, and to avoid anger. They are self-disciplined, work hard, and are responsible. They are conscious of duty, order, and improvement of the world.	Die to your perfectionism. With Christ as your source, you don't have to be perfect or always be right. You can forgive yourself and others for mistakes. It is okay to relax and enjoy yourself. You are worthy to ask for what you want and need. Be careful not to become harsh or judgmental when others don't meet your expectations.
Two. *The Giver (The Need to Be Needed).* Twos are motivated by the need to be loved and appreciated and to avoid being seen as needy. They are generous, warm, and caring. But they have a hard time saying no and rarely do things for themselves for fear of being selfish.	Die to your need to rescue others. It is God's work, not yours, to save the world. Die to your need for others to validate you and say you are okay. Die to the sin of pride in thinking you are indispensable. Be careful not to lose yourself in taking care of others. Be aware of the temptation of manipulation or possessiveness toward others. You don't have to give to be loved.

The Nine Enneagram Personality Types	What We Must Die To in Order for Christ to Become Our Source of Values and Self-Worth
Three. *The Achiever (The Need to Succeed).* Threes are motivated by the need to be productive, to achieve success, and to avoid failure. They are giving, responsible, and well-regarded by others. They are competent and hard working, goal-oriented, and good providers.	Die to your need to draw your sense of life and worth from your successes and your fear of making mistakes. Embrace God's rhythms of rest along with your work. Spend time hanging out with friends and family. Be aware of high expectations turning into an unhealthy perfectionism or unloving behavior. Because of Jesus' love, you can risk being vulnerable and weak.
Four. *The Romantic (The Need to Be Special).* Fours are motivated by the need to understand their feelings on a deep level and establish warm connections with others. They have active imaginations and creativity. They are on a constant search for the meaning of life and want to avoid appearing ordinary.	Die to your need to be extraordinary. Beware of the tendency to be envious or to fall into self-hatred, shame, or self-absorption. Be a thinker, and do not be entirely run by your feelings. Relax and enjoy the moment. You are the unique, beautiful, and beloved child of God, completely accepted by him.

The Nine Enneagram Personality Types	What We Must Die To in Order for Christ to Become Our Source of Values and Self-Worth
Five. *The Observer (The Need to Know)*. Fives are motivated by the need to know everything and understand the universe, giving them a sense of security. They avoid being dependent on others, preferring to remain emotionally disengaged.	Die to your need to withhold yourself from others. When you are in a group, be aware of the need to prove you know something. Let others know they are important to you. God is the source of your security and rest, not your knowledge. It is okay to make mistakes and not be the smartest person in a group.
Six. *The Dutiful (The Need for Security/Certainty)*. Sixes are motivated by the need for security, order, and certainty. They like to receive approval and be taken care of. They are very loyal and want to avoid being seen as rebellious.	Die to receiving approval from others and to the fear of the unknown. You can trust God is unchangeable and dependable. Be careful of being rigid, judgmental, defensive, and controlling. Develop a warm, intimate relationship with Jesus Christ and with those around you.

The Nine Enneagram Personality Types	What We Must Die To in Order for Christ to Become Our Source of Values and Self-Worth
Seven. *The Adventurer (The Need to Enjoy Life).* Sevens are motivated by the need to be happy and enjoy life. Enthusiasm, idealism, optimism, and joy radiate from them as they seek to contribute to the world. They seek to avoid suffering and pain.	Die to your avoidance of suffering, pain, and loss. Embracing loss is an integral part of the spiritual journey with Christ. Accept that life is hard as well as beautiful and that our joys are often sobered by sadness. Remember "there is a time for everything and a season for every activity under the heavens … a time to weep and a time to laugh, a time to mourn and a time to dance" (Ecclesiastes 3:1, 4) Your worth and value are in Christ alone, not feeling happy.
Eight. *The Asserter (The Need to Be Against).* Eights are motivated by the need to be against something, standing up for truth and justice. At times, they seek or create conflict. They are self-reliant and strong, desiring to make an impact on the world. They avoid appearing weak.	Die to your self-reliance and need to appear powerful and strong. Embrace weakness and vulnerability, especially the aspects of yourself that are soft and tender. Work on becoming safe and approachable for others. Loving relationships are more important than winning debates or arguments.

The Nine Enneagram Personality Types	What We Must Die To in Order for Christ to Become Our Source of Values and Self-Worth
Nine. *The Peacemaker (The Need to Avoid).* Nines are motivated by the need to keep the peace and to avoid conflict. They like to stay in the background and not be anything special. They are easygoing and don't draw attention to themselves.	Die to appeasing and giving in to others. Remember Christ disrupted false peace to bring true peace. Express your opinions and feelings. You have been given a life with talents and gifts that is important to give away. Because Jesus is your source and security, you can step out to act boldly and decisively.

The Enneagram is helpful in naming our root sins and mistaken attitudes, calling us to understand our gifts and primary sin tendencies. It uncovers the defense mechanisms that often develop in our family situations and personal circumstances. Most importantly, the Enneagram exposes aspects of our personality that separate us from God, others, and ourselves.

What I like about the Enneagram as a tool is the way it distinguishes our true self from the protective "false self" that we project to others. Take fifteen to thirty minutes to prayerfully reread the above chart. What number might best apply to you? Sit down with someone who knows you well over the next week and share this with them. Get feedback. Don't try to guess what other people are. That can only be done by each person in their own skin. You may want to pick up a book on the Enneagram, explore resources on the web, or attend a workshop to further explore this rich tool.

When we quit dying to the wrong things and begin the journey of knowing our hearts, our stories, and our personalities, we come alive to our true selves in Christ. As part of that process, we acknowledge and affirm the full range of human emotions — even those that are considered bad. We embrace all our humanity, realizing that the more we ignore or suppress certain emotions, the more we are controlled by them. This leads us to the next chapter, which deals with anger, sadness, and fear.

4

Quit Denying Anger, Sadness, and Fear

It was a very hot Fourth of July weekend, and we were in our early years of establishing New Life Fellowship Church.

"Hey, Geri, it is really important that we take advantage of this great weather. The park is going to be overflowing with people," Pete began. I knew what was coming. "So I am going to take out a group of people from New Life. I think it will be great for sharing Christ and helping people become aware of our church," he shared excitedly, almost as if I wasn't in the room.

"Well, I guess I could bring Maria and Christy and go along," I replied dejectedly. Our girls were only one and two at the time. Even as I made the suggestion, I knew it wouldn't work because both girls had different nap times. My dilemma was clear: I would pay a price if I went to the park with Pete, and I would pay a price if I stayed home.

Pete was quiet, so I answered for him, "No, it won't

work. We'll just stay home and figure out what to do for the day. You go."

"Great," he replied without hesitation. For Pete, it was simply another workday.

For me, the Fourth of July was a special day of fun, family, beach, friends, and barbeques. It was a holiday, not a work day. Pete didn't have to work that day, but he chose to. And I conceded.

I remained in Queens, in our second-floor apartment with no access to a backyard. I was now stuck indoors while my two young daughters took naps.

"Here I am in this hot, lonely apartment with two small kids while everyone else is celebrating a holiday," I whined to no one in particular.

Sadness enveloped me as the smell of neighboring barbeques floated up into our apartment. All I could think of was my family at the beach, swimming and having a delicious barbeque while I was confined to our small apartment.

I decided to call home. "Hi, Dad! How are the waves at the beach?" I asked.

"Oh, the water is beautiful and the waves are great. Everybody is at the beach! I'm the only one home right now. We wish you, Pete, and the girls were here." I fought back tears.

"What's up with you?" he asked.

I fought off the sadness. I ignored the hurt. I suppressed my anger.

"I'm home here with the girls. Today is a workday for Pete. He's at the park handing out fliers about our church."

Anger and sadness, so I thought, were not acceptable emotions for a good Christian, especially a good Christian pastor's wife.

When Pete returned that night, I asked him how it went, but I didn't really care. I hid my true feelings from him and even myself.

We moved on as if nothing happened.

Forbidden Emotions, Diminished People

That Fourth of July was just one of many days and many times I denied a very human part of me—my true feelings. I believed that those feelings were bad and that having them would make me bad.

Without even realizing what I was doing, I talked myself out of them: "Don't acknowledge those feelings. They aren't real. Eventually they'll disappear if you ignore them."

It had always been fairly easy for me to express excitement and enthusiasm openly. Yet, the difficult emotions such as anger, sadness, and fear were harder to manage. I felt guilty and ashamed for having them.

The ways we respond to certain emotions are directly related to how they were handled in our family of origin.

The ways we express and respond to certain emotions are directly related to how they were handled in our family of origin. If your parents or caregivers limited their range of thoughts and feelings, it naturally follows that your range of acceptable wishes and emotions is also restricted.

Children who are not allowed to express certain

feelings, over time, conclude, "Why feel those emotions in the first place?" Unwritten rules such as "a good girl always smiles in church," and "a loving person is never tense or suffering from unexplained depression," create real barriers that stifle authenticity and spontaneity in relationships.

Unfortunately, many church cultures reinforce this crippling approach, perpetuating a lifestyle in which we deal with distressing feelings in muddled and undifferentiated ways. In fact, most Christians I meet today actually feel unspiritual for attempting to sort out the source of their feelings.

As a young Christian, the Bible teaching I received emphasized joyfulness, overcoming obstacles, and being strong in Christ. Anger and sadness were acknowledged within the context of judging or praying for those who "struggled" with these troublesome emotions. I learned I was supposed to rejoice even if I was sad or angry. I certainly was not to share my fears since the Bible was filled with commands not to fear. These emotions were practically synonymous with sin. We imagined, or hoped, that by suppressing and ignoring them, they would somehow disappear.

How can the world know us when we don't truly know ourselves or one another?

This superficial and incomplete understanding of Scripture's view of our humanity almost destroyed me. At the least, it severely stunted my spiritual growth and ability to love well.

This tragic view also erodes any possibility of developing authentic Christian community. We build walls of separation and cannot truly see one another. We fear vulnerability and lie about what is going on inside us. Instead of inviting people to become more fully alive, we unintentionally create a religious subculture that constricts and deprives people from experiencing the full range of their God-given humanity. We mock the notion that the world will know Jesus by our love for one another (John 13:34–35). How can the world know us when we don't truly know ourselves or one another?

Emotional Illiteracy

Joan works part time, raises her two boys ages fourteen and twelve, and leads a mom's group at her church. She works hard on growing in Christ and taking care of herself. Sam, her husband, is highly intelligent, a civil engineer, and proud of his ability to think logically.

Joan is lonely in the marriage. Her misery is growing each year, yet she is afraid to admit this to herself, never mind her husband. Sam rationalizes away her distance and her negativity toward him. He tries to lose himself in his work and coaching his sons' soccer teams.

On the outside, Sam and Joan are a model Christian family. On the inside and behind closed doors, they remain deadlocked in an escalating cold war.

They are both emotionally illiterate. This is not uncommon for those of us who receive early training to distance ourselves from certain feelings, especially those that have to do with vulnerability, inadequacy, and weakness.

Joan works to portray the image of a woman who has it all together for the sake of Christ—both to her neighbors and extended family. Yet her anger and sadness leak out as sarcasm, mild depression, and a critical spirit. She remains busy at church and with her children. Sam senses no great need to address the tension as long as things remain stable at home.

What will it take for Joan and Sam to break through their pretense and acknowledge what is really going on? What will calm their fears and give them the courage to move forward in honesty?

There are many ways to answer these questions, but one thing is certain: Joan will have to stop denying her anger, sadness, and hurt. Her honesty will be essential for the future of their marriage and family.

What might it look like for Joan, and for you, to peer beneath the surface? What would happen if you really came to grips with your anger, sadness, and fear? How might this impact your relationship with Christ and with those around you?

One thing for sure does not survive such scrutiny: pretend spirituality. However, a deeper, powerful relationship with Christ, with ourselves, and with others now becomes a real possibility. But we must continue taking bold steps of faith. We must embrace the full range of our emotions, including the difficult and sometimes forbidden emotions of anger, sadness, and fear.

Anger

I have been confused about anger most of my life. As a child, I overtly blamed others. I complained and withdrew. As a Christian adult, however, I tried to suppress it because I believed all anger was bad. Yet . . .

- I was angry at Pete.
- I was angry at people in our church.
- I was angry at my neighbors.
- I was angry at my difficult circumstances.
- I was angry at my kids.
- I was angry at the poverty and need that surrounded me.
- I was angry at God for my hard life.
- I was angry at myself.
- I was angry at New York City—the parking tickets, traffic, the sanitation department that woke me up early every Saturday morning, and the building department that carelessly dismantled our neighborhood by converting single family homes into multiple-dwelling units.

For years, Pete and I were both struggling and stuck. Our marriage was unfulfilling, and spiritually we had hit a wall. The Christianity that had shaped us to that point was no longer working. Scared, confused, and desperate, we poured out our souls to a respected Christian counselor.

At the end of two hours the counselor turned to me and calmly said, "Geri, you have a lot of anger."

I was incredulous. So was Pete.

"Geri? I don't think so." Pete nervously defended me.

"Really," I finally responded, "I don't see it."

I was so unaware of my anger that it took two more years before I could begin to understand what the counselor was saying. Because I did not admit I was angry, I believed I wasn't. Of course, the counselor could easily observe the anger in my nonverbal cues — my tone of voice, sarcasm, and body language.

Like many followers of Christ, I did not believe I had permission to be angry. This left me feeling powerless, so I found other avenues for my anger. I complained. I blamed. I criticized. I defended myself. These outlets gave me the illusion of power.

How do you handle anger? How was anger expressed in your family when you were growing up? What words or phrases would you use to describe it? What happened when your parents were angry? How did you express anger toward a sibling? Your parents? As you watched anger expressed in your home, what decisions did you make about it? What happens to your body when you are around angry people? When you are angry now as an adult, how do you express it?

I had no idea anger could be used in a healthy way to assert oneself and to serve others. I also didn't realize I had a responsibility before God to process my anger, to think about it and respond appropriately. When I finally quit the lie that good Christians don't get angry, I walked through a door that changed my life.

When I finally quit the lie that good Christians don't get angry, I walked through a door that changed my life.

A word to those who have difficulty knowing when they're angry: you will want to watch your body closely. It will often reveal to you what is going on before your brain catches up. You may find your heart pumping faster, your pulse rate going up, or your neck, stomach, shoulders, and back tightening.

You may lose your appetite, become irritable, get tension headaches, or experience insomnia.

Anger is a vital, central discipleship issue for every Christian. It is a signal with many potential messages from God to us and a warning indicator light on life's dashboard, inviting us to stop and pay attention to our internal engine. And, believe it or not, anger often comes bearing gifts. Through anger, God may help us discover what we really want, get us to pay attention to even deeper emotions, help us identify unmet expectations, and, sometimes, see the folly of our sin.

Anger Can Be a Tool for Clarifying Values

My anger over our harried lifestyle was the impetus that enabled me to clarify the kind of marriage, family, and ministry I did—and did not—want.

Anger helps us know when our personal boundaries are being crossed. When this occurs, it forces me to ask the question, "What is being violated that is important to me?" If one of my daughters says to another, "That's a stupid comment," my value for a family that respects the thoughts and feelings of each person is violated. If Pete overworks and is emotionally unavailable, my value for the priority of time and energy needed for a healthy marriage is violated. When we are being disrespected, when too much of our self is being compromised in a relationship, when we are pressured to do more than we want to do, or when we say yes when we really mean no—our values or beliefs are being violated. It is a time to pause and reflect.

Anger Can Be a Signal of Deeper Emotions

It has been said that anger is a "secondary feeling." Anger often coexists with other feelings such as hurt, sadness, fear, disappointment, and shame. For this reason, exploring these deeper, more vulnerable emotions is essential to processing anger maturely.

When you are angry, ask yourself; What am I afraid of? Am I hurt?

When you are angry, it is important to ask yourself, "What am I afraid of? Am I hurt? Sad? Disappointed? What is really going on behind the anger?" When someone criticizes me, I become angry. My immediate instinct is to become defensive. But when I reflect on what is behind my anger, it is fear of inadequacy. I am not sure I am good enough. When Pete recently found out that one of his nephews got married without his brother calling him, he was very angry. He realized, however, that behind that anger was a profound sadness about the lack of closeness in his family.

For most people expressing anger feels less vulnerable than hurt or fear. For example, a person may be angry at a friend for forgetting their birthday, but what is really underneath the anger is hurt. Another person may be angry with their church for not doing enough social events for singles over thirty, only to discover that their anger is really covering a fear of being alone.

Anger Can Be an Indicator of Unmet Expectations

Next time you are angry, ask yourself: "What was I expecting?"

Unmet and unclear expectations in relationships,

whether in the family, workplace, classroom, friendships, dating relationships, or churches, are the source of much anger. We expect other people to know what we want before we are clear in our own minds or before we say it. Consider how you feel when someone is angry with you because you didn't fulfill their expectations, yet they never communicated this to you. They simply assumed you should know. The problem is that we have expectations that are unconscious (we are not even aware of them), unrealistic (we have illusions), unspoken (we keep them in our heads), and unagreed upon (the other person never said yes to them).

For example, you may become angry that your small group never socializes outside the regular meeting time. You had an expectation, yet you never spoke about this to the small-group leader. You may be angry at your spouse for not calling you each day from work. You believed they should just know to call you. But you never asked them to do so. I remember being angry at my daughters for leaving their shoes in the front hallway of our house each day after school. My anger was due to my own faulty assumption that they should just know to put them away in the front closet without my telling them. I never spoke the expectation. But I sure did yell.

When you understand you don't have a right to many of your expectations because they have not been spoken or agreed upon, you will find you carry much less anger.

Anger Can Be a Sin

Anger may reveal pettiness, arrogance, hatred, envy, or a desire to hurt someone else. Pay attention to any sarcastic or caustic remarks you make. Pay attention if you find yourself avoiding someone. You may be jealous of another person's promotion at work. Your anger may be a result of your anxiety and projection. When you are angry about something and then take it out on someone who has nothing to do with it, that is sinful.

Since anger is such a complex emotion, I have found it helpful to ask myself the following questions to help me process it before taking any action steps: Is this misplaced blame for which I need to take responsibility? Is my anger justifiable or is it coming from the worst in me? Is there anyone from whom I need to ask forgiveness for wounding with my anger?

Aristotle rightly said, "Anyone can be angry, that is easy ... but to be angry with the right person, to the right degree, at the right time, for the right purpose, and in the right way ... this is not easy."[1]

It is easy to be angry and not take responsibility for it. Acknowledging anger so you can process it properly and not project it on to others is a huge step in spiritual and emotional maturity. At the end of this chapter, after exploring sadness and fear, we will consider three simple guidelines for processing our emotions in a way that keeps us centered on God and his will.

Sadness

If emotions can be teachers sent from God, it is perhaps the family of feelings around sadness—loneliness, hurt, discouragement, depression, gloominess—that are the greatest teachers of all. They formed passageways that led me into hidden truths about myself and God, and I have become a much more avid student of these emotions as a result.

My relationship with sadness was as inhumane and unbiblical as my relationship with anger. When feelings of sadness arose, I quickly covered over them and moved on. They were inhumane because I denied the pain that comes with living in a fallen world. I allowed myself to feel only the happy parts of my life. In doing so, I was, in effect, half human. This also kept me from identifying with a common brokenness shared by all people on the earth.

The problem was that I had a lot to be sad about. This included a marriage in which I functioned as a solo parent for the first eight years; I could not get those years back. Our children had grown up in a place where it was dangerous to ride their bikes. They had to travel long distances to school, resulting in friendships far from our neighborhood. In the twenty-five-plus years Pete and I have led our community at New Life Fellowship Church, many people left or moved away. People changed; we changed. Relationships changed.

I picked up an unspoken rule both growing up and in my spiritual formation: "To be sad is to be weak. And to be weak is bad." I loved the Bible verses: "The joy of the LORD is your strength," and "I can do all this through him who gives me strength" (Nehemiah 8:10; Philippians 4:13). For me they translated into: "You know you have enough faith if you are happy all the time, regardless of the circumstances."

So when I found myself flat on my back in depression during our fifth year of marriage, struggling to get out of bed to care for two small children, I was stunned. I tried to will myself out of the sadness, but I couldn't.

"A broken leg would be easier to fix than this, whatever this is," I complained.

I couldn't fix my broken spirit. Pete prayed. Leaders from the church prayed. I remained depressed.

My depression was a signal to pay attention to my inner pain, but my faulty theology won out. With much effort, I shook it off and returned to my relentless schedule and to denying the truth of my emotional condition.

When the depression returned the following year, I shrugged it off again. "Depression runs in my family," I reassured myself. "I will just have to fight through these thorns in the flesh the rest of my life." My unyielding sadness, I wrongly believed, was holding me back. It prevented me from continuing as the strong Christian that God intended. I resented the weakness I could not escape.

God and Our Losses

We tend to view our losses as alien invaders that interrupt our "normal" lives. Yet loss is a part of life. People we love die. Relationships are severed. Doors close. Dreams are dashed. We relocate. We say good-bye to a church or community. Abuse robs us of our innocence. We accomplish a goal and have to say farewell to a process that got us there. We age and lose our health. Our children grow up. Over the span of our lives, we will leave everything behind.

We don't know how to talk about sadness or disappointments. So we get busy and seek ways to medicate our pain. We escape into shopping, working, watching

TV, food binges, drugs or alcohol, fantasies or pornography, email, and Facebook.

In many churches the unspoken rule is this: "You aren't spiritual if you're feeling depressed or sad." So people pretend that all is well. The not-so-subtle message is that good Christians aren't supposed to feel hurt, confused, or discouraged.

Yet the Bible affirms the human experience and expression of sadness and grief. Jesus, our Lord and Savior, was a man of sorrows, familiar with pain (Isaiah 53:3). He offered up prayers with loud cries and tears (Hebrews 5:7). We observe him in the Garden of Gethsemane before going to the cross, struggling with the will of the Father. The Bible describes him as "being in anguish, he prayed more earnestly, and his sweat was like drops of blood falling to the ground" (Luke 22:44). Jesus, our Messiah and God, did not deny his sadness and anguish.

David is well-known for being a man after God's own heart. Yet two-thirds of his psalms are laments or complaints. Joseph, who was favored by God, exhibits no shame at weeping loudly before his brothers. Jeremiah protested to God about his circumstances at least six different times and wrote Lamentations, an entire book that expresses his deep anguish to God over the destruction of Jerusalem.

Scripture ... considers grieving losses as central to our spiritual growth.

Scripture does more than give us permission to express our sadness; it considers grieving losses as central to our spiritual growth. Sadness and loss form important threads in the tapestry of our spiritual lives. We are to grieve parents who were not there for us, severed relationships, lack of education, lack of job opportunities, divorces, deaths, disabilities, challenging children, chronic health limitations, and childlessness. To deny sadness is like trying to deny an arm or a leg; it is to amputate a vital and necessary part of ourselves.

Making Peace

I used to fear sadness as if it were a contagious disease. Now that I allow myself to experience sadness, the fear of it has lost its grip on me. I no longer label sadness as bad or something to be avoided; it is simply a part of life.

Experiencing my own sadness has enabled me to be more compassionate toward the sadness of others. I am now convinced this is one of the greatest gifts I have to offer. Think about it. How can you enter into the pain of others if you have not entered into your own? How can you offer the comfort of Jesus Christ if you have not experienced it yourself?

Experiencing our sadness is one of the greatest gifts I have to offer.

It doesn't matter how much you read your Bible, do good works, go to church, serve others, or know about God. If you are not honest about your true feelings, you will be stunted in your spiritual growth with God and limited in your relationships.

When we accept all our emotions, we protect ourselves from needless inner conflict between what we are truly feeling and the voices telling us that we shouldn't feel those things. When we accept all our emotions, it is the beginning of making peace with ourselves.

You are allowed to be sad over disappointments and

losses of people or things that matter to you. Pause for a few moments. "Be still before the LORD" (Psalm 37:7). Let any thoughts or feelings rise to the surface as you consider the following questions: What are some things you are sad about? What are a few of the losses you are carrying from this past year? What setbacks or disappointments are impacting you? How might God be speaking or shaping you through these things? Offer them one by one to God.

Fear

"Pete, you didn't finish the dishes yet!" I flippantly remarked as I walked in the door.

"Geri," Pete kindly began, "When you said that, did you catch your tone?"

He was right. I remained silent.

In the previous few weeks, Pete had begun to hold me accountable for my sharp, condescending tone of voice. This forced me to acknowledge how scared I was to admit my faults and to be vulnerable. The Holy Spirit spoke to me, "Geri, you murder Pete with that tone of voice. He is made in my image, and it is terribly disrespectful to be condescending to another human being."

I was afraid to admit my flaws. I don't like being exposed for who I really am on the inside. To be thought of as less than perfect did not fit my image as a good and loving person. I was frightened in being exposed as judgmental and murderous.

Pete gave me a gift when he confronted me. That day marked a new beginning for me to admit my fears. I felt very weak and exposed. Yet I heard God's voice in my inner person say, "You're lovable, Geri. Just rest in my love." The great news of Jesus Christ is that, in the gospel, he loves us without any strings attached. There is nothing left to prove.

Surprisingly, I didn't "die" or "crack." Instead I experienced tremendous relief, even a sense of renewed freedom and power. A powerful chain that held me my entire life was finally broken.

Examining the root of our fears is important spiritual work. Fears about our value, worth, and lovability surface that are crucial for our transformation into the love and freedom God longs to grant to us.

Facing Our Fears

Perhaps the most repeated command in the Bible is "Do not fear." So doesn't it seem natural that we should suppress fear? Isn't fear something we are called to do away with? The answer is both yes and no.

The Bible does not say that we are not to have feelings of fear. In fact, Scripture commands us to know our hearts, to examine closely the roots of our fears and anxieties. Fear is a natural response to perceived threats and dangers. Our hearts begin to beat faster, and our stomachs tighten. We experience fear when we take exams, we start a new job, we lose a job, or a car turns sharply toward us on a street corner. Sadly, many of us feel guilty and weak admitting our fears, so we avoid acknowledging them, hoping they will somehow go away. In doing so we give them more, not less, power.

While there are a myriad of fears, researcher and psychologist Michael Yapko's thirty-year study on fear identifies three general categories.[2] It behooves us to become aware of which one most drives our behavior. Unhealthy fears restrict and narrow us in powerful ways, causing us to make poor, reactive decisions. They impact how we parent our children, approach our relationships, choose to remain or change jobs, and handle our finances.

The first category of fear relates to *the fear of making mistakes.* People who fear making mistakes are often perfectionists who dread disappointing themselves and others. They fear criticism—real or imagined. That fear drives them to make unrealistic expectations of themselves and others.

The second category relates to *the fear of rejection.* People who fear rejection are afraid to join a new small group, initiate conversation with a boss or pastor, or raise their hand in a classroom to ask a question lest they expose themselves as inadequate in some way. The very thought of other people judging them informs many of their decisions.

The third category afflicts people who *fear consequences from relaxing.* They maintain a vigilant and defensive posture through life out of fear that someone, or something, will hurt them. They have a difficult time letting their guard down.

We are not to deny our fears. In fact, God invites us to identify them and, by the power of his Spirit, move through them. Scripture is filled with powerful examples of people moving through their fears.

- At the age of eighty, Moses moved through his fear of self-doubt and inferiority to confront Pharaoh.

- David moved through the fears of those around him who said he could not succeed in battle with Goliath.

- Esther, a Jewish queen, moved through her fear of losing her life by breaking an entrenched social taboo and approaching her husband, the king of Persia.

- Joseph, Jesus' earthly father, moved through his fears of shame and humiliation when he said yes to God and married Mary.

Each biblical example teaches us that courage is not the absence of fear. Instead, it is the capacity to think and act despite our fears, to step over them because of a larger God-vision. Unacknowledged fears can be a powerful force that constricts us. Unless we step over our fears through faith in Jesus, we will inevitably remain stuck in our spiritual lives, our marriages, and our futures.

What might happen if you moved through your fears?

Imagine the possibilities for your life if you knew you could make mistakes, be imperfect, and still be loved. What might you attempt if you didn't depend on your performance to receive love from others? What would you do for God with your talents and gifts if you knew that, even if you failed, it was okay? What might you do if you were so secure in the love of God that you were free from the approval of others? What would you do if you were free to speak the truth to people around you?

What might happen if you moved through your fears?

When I finally admitted I had a fear of being weak, I moved through it by turning to God's love. I listened to God's voice and received his love during intentional times of silence and Scripture reading. I paid attention to what was happening in the movements of my heart, revealing where I was depending on the approval of people for my value and worth instead of God's all-encompassing love.

Fear comes with being human. Pause for a few moments in God's presence. Ask yourself the following questions: What are you afraid of? What are you anxious about? Money? Security? Children? Spouse? Relationships? Work? Future? Health? Meditate on the truth of Psalm 46:10: "Be still, and know that I am God." Along with this, gather data to ensure you are accurately informed concerning your fears—that might include a health checkup, talking with a mature person about how to address the tensions in your marriage, or meeting with a consultant about your finances. And finally, formulate a specific plan of action to actually step over that fear.

Three Guidelines to Quit Denying Anger, Sadness, and Fear

Here are three simple guidelines to help you process your feelings of anger, sadness, and fear: feel your feelings, think through your feelings, and then take the appropriate action.

Feel Your Feelings

When it comes to feelings, we need to avoid the extremes—we should neither neglect our emotions nor allow them to run our lives. We don't want to put them in either the trunk or the driver's seat. Rather, we want to care for them so that they serve us.

To feel means to be aware of your emotions and to acknowledge them. Allow yourself to experience them without self-condemnation. Explore them in the presence of God, who loves you.

One way to develop awareness of feelings is to keep a journal. This was a foundational discipline for me as I began to exercise long dormant "feeling" muscles. Three to four times a week, I paused to reflect on the feelings I had experienced that day. During those "feeling" workouts in my journal, I began to strengthen my awareness of what I was truly feeling. Over time, I got better at identifying my feelings in the moment so I didn't have to wait until later to acknowledge and express them. I also experienced greater freedom and peace from inner turmoil because I was no longer suppressing or devaluing myself.

Scripture invites us to express our feelings to God: "Trust in him at all times, you people; pour out your hearts to him" (Psalm 62:8). Unfortunately, many of us have been socialized to pour out our hearts to no one. Even the people closest to us know us only partially and imperfectly. But God is totally trustworthy and safe. We can be entirely open with him. We can pour out our hearts to him because nothing, absolutely nothing, can cause God to withhold his love from us.

One day Pete called me saying our friend Julius had asked for a last-minute meeting. Pete asked if I objected to him working late that evening. My neck and shoulders tightened; my heartbeat quickened. But I said, "Sure. Come home late. Dinner will be ready. I don't mind." And I returned to the tasks of the day.

Later that day, while reflecting and journaling my feelings, I became aware that I had lingering feelings of anger and irritation around Pete's requests and my response.

Now I was ready for the second step in the process of quitting the denial of my emotions, namely, to think through feelings.

Think through Your Feelings

As I thought about my response to Pete's request on the phone, I became aware I said yes because I didn't want to appear selfish. I realized I wasn't bad for wanting him to be home on time. I can value myself enough to say, "I want and need your help around dinnertime with our four young children." I also recognized how important it was for me that we have dinner together as a family each night, and that was a valid desire that I needed to express clearly to Pete.

Henri Nouwen once remarked that we ought to spend 50 percent of our time living our lives and the other 50 percent reflecting on what is being lived.[3] Thinking is an ability given solely to human beings made in God's image. This gift enables us to respond to our feelings thoughtfully rather than to react hastily. We are to feel our feelings, but we are not always to follow them. The writer of Proverbs states that "desire without knowledge is not good—how much more will hasty feet miss the way" (Proverbs 19:2). We will talk more about this in chapter 7 on faulty thinking.

After you identify your feelings, ask yourself, "What are the reasons I am feeling this way?" For example, you are anxious for tomorrow's meeting with your boss. Once you acknowledge that fear, you may be asking yourself:

What is this about? What if he fires me? What if he lowers my salary and I can't support myself any longer?

After thinking about what you are feeling—whether it be sadness, anger, or fear—you are ready for the third simple step of taking action.

Take Appropriate Action

Once I realized I had lied to Pete about his coming home late, saying yes when I really meant no, the question now remained, "What, Geri, is the appropriate action step?" I was tempted to blame him for making an insensitive request. Why couldn't he just say no to Julius who wanted so desperately to meet with him? Didn't Pete understand how it was impacting me?

I calmed down and realized blaming him was not a good action step. How could he know what was going on inside me unless I told him? I decided not to wait for him to come home to have the conversation. After I finished journaling, I called him back and honestly shared my true feelings and desires. Without any fanfare, he simply responded, "Thanks, honey, for letting me know. Of course! See you at 6:00."

I went through much struggle and anguish to process my thoughts and feelings around this incident. What I gained, however, in terms of spiritual formation in Christ was priceless. I stopped lying. I valued myself. I esteemed my marriage. I learned to relate to God in new ways.

At times, the appropriate action step will be clear. Say no to that invitation. Step over your fear and take that job opportunity. Wait before committing to this new relationship.

In other situations, discerning the appropriate action step takes considerable time. You may need time to gather more information and think through alternatives. It may, for example, involve key conversations you want to have about a decision. You may want to consult with a trusted friend. You may need extended time alone with God. You may realize your need to learn new skills, such as mature speaking and listening, fighting fairly, or clarifying expectations.

You may have had ten, twenty, thirty, or fifty years of handling anger, sadness, and fear in ways that are both unbiblical and damaging to your soul. Give yourself grace and time as you learn this process.[4]

To quit denying sadness, anger, and fear will lead you to a more mature and healthy life—emotionally, physically, and spiritually. Owning your feelings will also prevent you from projecting your emotions on to others in poisonous ways. This naturally leads us to our next chapter about our need to quit blaming and to take responsibility for our lives.

5

Quit Blaming

When Pete and I married, the two of us became one—and he was the one! Instead of creating space for both of us to flourish, the marriage created a hole into which I somehow fell and disappeared.

It was natural to lose myself in Pete's life. He seemed to know more clearly what he wanted. I went along when Pete wanted to vacation in Nicaragua—in the middle of their civil war—while I was six months pregnant, even though this wasn't my idea of rest and relaxation. I followed Pete to New York City to plant a church—without parishioners, a facility, or money—even though I wondered if we were better off waiting. I immersed myself in Pete's workaholic pace of life even though I was tired and increasingly lonely. I adopted Pete's strong opinion that I should stay in Queens with our young children during the long, hot summers even though I longed to be with my parents near the beach in New Jersey.

As I look back on the many ways I lost myself in Pete's life, I do not blame him. Of course, I did at the time.

Although he had blind spots about what was driving his behavior, he was not responsible for my choices. I was *fully* responsible for allowing Pete to cross so many of my personal boundaries and to ignore my desire for a different kind of life. I mistakenly believed I was powerless to change my many frustrating life situations. The best I could do was to blame Pete and others as life happened to me.

The Blame Game

Blaming, sad to say, has always been with us. Adam blamed Eve. Eve blamed the serpent. Sarah blamed Hagar. Joseph's brothers blamed him. The Israelites blamed Moses. Moses blamed God. Saul blamed David.

Blaming comforts us, at least for a while, with the illusion that we are in control.

Today, when things don't go our way, we blame our parents, spouses, children, schools, government, corporations, bosses, employees, leaders, weather patterns, inflation, traffic. We blame demonic powers, even God himself when things are really bad.

Blaming comforts us, at least for a while, with the illusion that we are in control. However, it actually accomplishes the opposite, stripping us of our God-given personal power and keeping us helplessly stuck in immaturity.

Here are examples of comments that demonstrate how we sometimes play the blame game in order to avoid taking responsibility for our lives:

- "You are ruining my life."
- "My boss makes my life miserable. I wish I could work somewhere else."
- "The church is not meeting my needs."
- "I am exhausted because my spouse won't take a vacation."
- "It is because my job doesn't pay enough that I have so much debt."
- "I'm not growing spiritually because the church is so immature."
- "Credit card companies are ruining my life."
- "My relationship with my fiancé is so bad because he won't go to counseling."
- "It's too late for me to change jobs."
- "I'm a single mom. I'll be poor the rest of my life."
- "Whenever I visit my parents for the holidays, they stress me out."
- "I've never been able to do science or math. I had terrible teachers."

Blaming statements can give the illusion of helplessness. We mistakenly believe we don't have choices. Yet blaming undermines the blamer in insidious ways. When blamers play the victim, they often retain a sense of moral superiority over others. In doing so, they disown responsibility. We observe this in the Garden of Eden where Adam and Eve attempted to gain the upper hand through blaming one another. Blamers are typically angry and preoccupied with what others *should* be doing rather than facing their own discomfort. This is easier, at least in the short term, than making the difficult choices they face.

When we continue to let hurtful situations go on

hurting us or accept pain because we "have to," we wrongly interpret our lives as out of our control. We think we are victims of our circumstances. As a result, we can often end up depressed.

The following are six signs that indicate you may be using blame to avoid personal responsibility:

1. You feel you have been dealt a "bad hand" in life.
2. You don't think you can change anything in your life for the better.
3. You view negative occurrences and relationships in your life as being out of your control.
4. You rarely believe you are wrong.
5. You think apologizing is a sign of weakness.
6. You dwell on the past instead of looking to the future.

If you find yourself blaming others and feeling like a victim, it is time to ask an important question: "What am I going to do about it?" Asking yourself this question shifts the focus from blaming others to taking personal responsibility for your life.

Take Responsibility for Your Life

You do have choices. No one is responsible for you and your life but you.

If your spouse doesn't want to go out, you can go out on your own or with friends. If you hate driving an hour a day to work, look for a new job closer to home or move closer to your job. If parents are difficult to be around and refuse to change, you are free to determine the boundar-

ies of *when, how,* or even *if* you want to spend time with
them. Maybe your spouse will not go to counseling to
work on your marriage, but you can go yourself to work
on your own blockages in the relationship. You may be
blaming the credit card company for causing you a great
deal of stress by calling you multiple times a day. Instead
of avoidance, you can locate a financial counselor or organization to create a plan to dig
yourself out of your financial hole, learn
money management skills, and establish long-
term stability.

> *No one is responsible for you and your life but you.*

Cynthia has been married to Jackson for
eighteen years. Throughout their married life, she has
cooked all the meals for him and their three children. "I
hate cooking and being responsible for cleaning up after
the meals. It's not fair," she complained year after year.
She mistakenly assumed it was her duty as a faithful wife.
She resented Jackson for this, and it leaked out in sarcastic
remarks and distancing.

Cynthia was then part of a small group at church
where she began to grow and learn about valuing herself. "I finally stopped blaming my husband," she told me,
"because I recognized it was my responsibility to speak up
and declare my preferences. I had to be willing to rock the
boat if necessary."

Actually, Cynthia's husband was more than willing
to divide up their cooking and cleanup responsibilities.
Cynthia had never asked. This proved to be a simple but
profound life lesson for her as she moved from blaming to
taking responsibility for her preferences and needs.

Michele carried deep pain because of a difficult sexual

relationship with her husband, Bill. "If he would just change," she thought, "everything would be wonderful." She prayed God would "fix him" and make things right. It didn't happen. One year turned to five. Five years turned to ten.

"Eventually," Michele lamented, "my anger and pain turned into depression until God finally met me. He showed me I was part of the problem . . . and that our sexual difficulties were a symptom of all the other unhealthiness in our marriage."

Michele made a decision to take responsibility for her own issues, her own happiness, and their need for professional intervention. "God did redeem the mess we made of our relationship," she recounted. "It took years of courage, honesty, hard work, and taking responsibility for ourselves. But we now enjoy an intimacy and safety in our sexual relationship that I couldn't have imagined when I was begging God to 'fix him.'" Her husband later expressed deep gratitude that Michele had stopped blaming him for their sexual problems and had never given up hope.

Discover Your God-Given Personal Freedom Kit

In the great classic *The Wizard of* Oz, Dorothy, the Scarecrow, the Tin Man, and the Lion are all looking for something outside themselves to set them free. Dorothy wants to go home, the Scarecrow is looking for a brain, the Tin Man wants a heart, and the Lion is looking for courage.

After a long, frustrating journey, they finally arrive at

their destination only to make a surprising discovery. The qualities they thought only the Wizard could give them were, in fact, qualities they already possessed; they simply needed to be reminded to take the risky step of putting those things to use. Immediately after being told he had a brain, the Scarecrow started making mathematical computations. The Tin Man's ticking heart affirmed the ability he had to love others. The Cowardly Lion, after receiving a medal of courage, rediscovered his bravery. And Dorothy realized she had always had the power to go home; her trials taught her the importance of her family, and she finally chose for herself to go home. No other person could have done that for her.

In a similar way, as human persons created in God's image, we are born with certain rights and responsibilities that enable us to walk in God-given personal freedom (Genesis 1:26–31). We don't need, for example, to find someone else to give us permission to make choices, set boundaries, declare preferences, think for ourselves, or feel; these abilities are already ours. However, like the characters in Oz, we have to take responsibility for what we've been given and put those things to use. This includes the freedom to take responsibility for choosing our own lives.

Personal Freedom Toolkit

After years of working to reclaim the freedom to choose my own life and helping others to do the same, I've developed what I call the Personal Freedom Toolkit.[1] This is my adaptation and expansion of a toolkit created by well-known psychologist Virginia Satir. The nine tools in the kit are essential if we are to quit blaming others and take responsibility for our own lives. Each tool reminds us of a right or responsibility as human beings made in God's image and as followers of Jesus Christ. The following list gives you an overview of these simple but life-changing tools. They are easy to learn but challenging to practice:

These tools include:

- The Fence of Separateness (Practice boundaries)
- The Voice of Declaration (Speak up)
- The Yes/No Medallion (Say yes or no)
- The Heart of Feelings (Pay attention to feelings)
- The Oxygen Mask of Self-Care (Take care of yourself)
- The Mirror of Self-Confrontation (Confront yourself)
- The Key of Hope (Remain hopeful)
- The Hat of Wisdom (Think carefully)
- The Badge of Courage (Be courageous)

1. The Fence of Separateness

Fences are boundaries; they enable us to know where our yard ends and our neighbor's yard begins. In the Bible, boundaries are evidenced from the beginning of creation. To bring order out of chaos, God separates the earth from the sky, the water from the land, night from day.

God also created human beings with boundaries. The word *existence* comes from a word meaning to *stand apart.*[2] Before there were two people in the garden, there was one. Adam and Eve each had an identity as a unique human being apart from the other. Their identities as separate individuals were crucial for their healthy togetherness.

In the same way, God gives us boundaries so we know where we end and others begin. These boundaries include our own thoughts, feelings, hopes, dreams, fears, values, and beliefs. These things set us apart, reminding us of our separateness as individuals. When I let someone, for example, pressure me into doing something I don't agree with or don't want to do, I allow my boundaries to be crossed.

Skin is an example of an important personal boundary. Your skin, and everything in it, belongs to you and no one else. You are in charge of your body, whether you are married or single. You are to respect it and make sure that others respect it. Far too many people, especially women, allow the boundary of their skin to be violated. If someone crosses your skin boundary in a way that makes you feel uncomfortable, you have the right and responsibility to say no.

In addition to establishing and enforcing our own boundaries, we must respect the boundaries of others. We do this by valuing differences. When our opinions or ideas are different, we must respect the choices others make, even if they are vastly different than ours. We do not belittle or demonize them. We violate the fence of separateness when we tell people what they should think and feel. We utter boundary-crossing statements such as:

- "That's ridiculous, how could you think that?"
- "You shouldn't be angry."
- "I can't believe you liked that movie!"
- "You don't care about me. That's why you don't call me."

The Fence of Separateness is a simple but powerful tool that enables us to respond differently in situations that used to make us feel helpless. Instead of being afraid to speak up and assert ourselves, or losing ourselves in someone else's life, we claim our freedom as distinct individuals and express our own thoughts and feelings. Now, when we feel disrespected at work, instead of just allowing it to happen, we may say, "Mr. Jones, I don't appreciate it when you correct me in front of others. I would prefer that you speak to me in private."

If you have difficulty establishing boundaries, perhaps you never saw them modeled or practiced. You may have experienced sexual, physical, or emotional abuse in your home growing up. Establishing a Fence of Separateness will require God's power, a near-heroic level of courage, and support from others. Get help. You can learn this. You are worth it.

Remember: If people cross our boundaries, it is because we allow it. No one but you is responsible to ensure your boundaries are respected.

2. The Voice of Declaration

This tool is indispensable for asserting your God-given separateness. By *voice* I mean our ability to speak on our own behalf, to be able to tell others what we think and feel.

Declaring oneself is challenging for those who grew up with unspoken rules that said something like, "It's not polite to ask for what you want or need," or "Don't say anything unpleasant out loud." Perhaps your father taught you not to swear but swore himself. The unspoken rule in your home was, "Don't talk about Dad's hypocrisy." Or maybe you were not allowed to mention a parent's excessive drinking or rage or depression. Nobody was to talk about it. You learned that using your voice—speaking your truth out loud—was dangerous.

Now that you are an adult, however, there isn't anyone else but you who can articulate your wants and needs or speak your truth. No one is an expert on you but you. If you don't voice your needs, preferences, and what is important to you, no one else can—or should. You alone are responsible for being clear, honest, and respectful in declaring yourself.

It's important to note that when you speak on your own behalf, you are not speaking *against* others but *for* yourself. Sometimes we think that people who do not agree with us are against us. This is not true. They merely have a different opinion. If I disagree with your convictions about global warming, the economy, or gay marriage, my purpose is not to be antagonistic or difficult. I am simply being true to my own values and convictions. If

> No one is an expert on you but you.

I tell Pete I prefer time alone this evening, it is not against him. I love and enjoy his company. I simply must first recharge my emotional batteries in order to love him well. If I say no to your invitation to a movie, it is nothing personal. I prefer to stay home and rest my tired body.

Declaring my own needs and preferences is something I still have to work at. I recently used a gift certificate to enjoy a therapeutic massage, one of my favorite ways to relax and take care of myself. During the massage, I began to experience pain in my shoulder because of the awkward position of my head and neck. When I asked the massage therapist for a pillow to raise my head, she suggested I wait a few minutes until after she finished massaging my neck. However, when the pain worsened, I asserted myself more strongly, "Please, I need a pillow. I am in a lot of pain."

As the massage continued, I realized the therapist wasn't applying the deep pressure I needed in order to release the tension in my neck and shoulders. I thought to myself, "Do I dare assert myself a third time? I don't want to be a complainer." Then I said to myself, "No, Geri, you have a right to declare yourself. This massage is a gift you want to enjoy and she's being paid for her work."

I did ask for more pressure, which the therapist was more than happy to give, but it was another reminder of how difficult it can be, even in everyday situations, to pull the Voice of Declaration out of the toolbox.

Our daily lives are filled with opportunities and challenges to declare ourselves—or to shrink back out of fear or guilt. For example:

- "I prefer to sit in a different spot at the restaurant than where we are seated."
- "We won't be traveling to your home this Christmas. We have chosen to stay home."
- "I don't like it when you drive above the speed limit around curves. I don't feel safe."
- "I value the environment so I am going to stop buying bottled water for our family."
- "I'd like to pause. I don't think this haircut is turning out the way I expected."

- "I would like to ask you not to check your email while we are in a meeting."
- "I do not want to go to that event. I prefer to stay home."
- "What exactly is the salary and benefits package for this job? Is that negotiable?"

When we use our voices to declare ourselves, we are not trying to control or manipulate others. We are speaking with an attitude of deep respect both for ourselves and others. Our words don't carry anger or a defensive tone.

We also use our voice to make comments or express puzzlement about things that are confusing. We have the right to ask hard questions even when it is uncomfortable.

God has a voice. He speaks. As God's child, made in his image, you too have a voice and are called to use it in loving yet powerful ways. It is your Voice of Declaration, and you can't live your unique, God-given life without it.

3. The Yes/No Medallion

Two words are especially important in the Personal Freedom Toolkit: *yes* and *no*. Both words are powerful, and both pose unique challenges.

Many of us feel guilty saying no. We want to be liked and not disappoint people, and perhaps we imagine that saying no is somehow less than Christlike. But consider Jesus' example and whether or not he disappointed people.

- He said no to the crowds who wanted to make him king (John 6:14–16).
- He said no to Peter who wanted him to avoid the cross (Matthew 16:21–23).

- He said no to the religious leaders who wanted him to stop claiming to be the Messiah (John 9:35–39).
- He said no to his family who wanted him to return home (Mark 3:31–34).
- He said no to the people who wanted him to come down off the cross to prove he was the Son of God (Luke 23:35–39).

If Jesus did not say no because of a fear of disappointing people, he would not have fulfilled the mission and the purpose God gave him. He would have lived up to other people's expectations instead of his own. Exercising a healthy no is essential if we are to fulfill the Father's destiny for our own lives as well.

It's important to understand that both *yes* and *no* are loving words. Remember, when I say no, it is not *against* you but *for* me. And while my no may make you sad, it doesn't make me bad. Most importantly, if I say yes when I prefer to say no, I erode my integrity and hurt both of us. Saying no, when appropriate, is the right of every adult:

- "No, I can't help you today."
- "No, I can't watch the kids this Saturday."
- "No, I won't be coming over this week."
- "No, I won't be accepting your invitation this time."
- "No, I don't want to give your friend a ride home tonight."

We must be able to say no if we are to say a healthy yes. A healthy yes comes from a sincere heart that both desires and is able to do something. It is infused with delight, without strings attached and absent of any resentment:

- "Yes, feel free to call me anytime today."
- "Yes, I'm happy to give you a ride to the store."
- "Yes, I will be glad to drive to the conference."
- "Yes, I look forward to being with you tomorrow night."
- "Yes, I can watch your children so you can get some time alone."

> *We must be able to say no if we are to say a healthy yes.*

Imagine wearing the Yes/No Medallion around your neck this week. As you are presented with choices and decisions, take the medallion in your hand, turning it to *yes* or *no*, whichever is the right choice for you.

4. The Heart of Feelings

The heart tool reminds me that I need to take regular time to pay attention to the feelings going on inside me. They are important indicators and ways that God comes to me. The events, people, and things that excite emotion in me are part of what makes me a unique human being. When I am aware, for example, of what gives my soul joy and life, I am more apt to assert myself and pursue those things that bring me pleasure and joy.

I paid attention to my anger when Pete accepted phone calls during dinner. Instead of using my anger to blame him—"You don't spend time with me and the kids!"—I listened to it and recognized it for what it was: a warning that something I valued was being violated. I was then able to assert myself: "Pete, I'd like you to silence your cell phone during dinner so we can have uninterrupted family time."

Using this tool means I acknowledge my disappointments and sadness. This can range from disappointment with poor food at a restaurant on a special night out, to the disillusionment when not hired for a highly sought-after job appointment. For years I carried the faulty belief that to be disappointed was to be ungrateful, and to be ungrateful was to be bad. Chronic complaining projects anxiety outward toward others. I learned, however, that admitting disappointment humbly reveals and opens our hearts. It involves vulnerability, not entitlement, creating an atmosphere in which God opens our hearts and meets us.

Using the Heart of Feelings tool also involves acknowledging my happiness. One summer I was flooded with energy and joy as I stepped out of our car into a family resort camp in the mountains for our vacation. For the next week, I reveled in hiking, swimming, sailing, kayaking, watercolor lessons, beauty, and being with family. My deep joy alerted me to changes I wanted to make in both our vacations and our lifestyle.

Spend time each day asking yourself, "How am I feeling? What am I angry about? Sad about? Anxious about? Glad about?" Journal, and then ask, "How is God speaking to me through these feelings?"

5. The Oxygen Mask of Self-Care

When traveling on a plane with a child, you are instructed that in the unlikely event of an emergency, you are to put on your own oxygen mask before helping a child with theirs. Why? Because she who is not breathing herself cannot help anyone else! A famous proverb puts it this way,

"She who is not happy cannot help very many people." In other words, I must first take care of myself if I want to provide care to others.

Applying the Oxygen Mask of Self-Care means doing things that refresh you and give you life. This means being in touch with your wishes and dreams, the things that cause you to feel fully alive. As author Parker Palmer has asked, "Is the life I am living the same as the life that God wants to live in me?" It is easy to live a life other than your own, to slip into meeting other people's expectations for your life. Over time, this slowly erodes the time available for you to spend on your own life. Are you only spending time doing things others want you to do? Or do you regularly include activities that you love to do?

Pete and I have been at New Life Fellowship Church in Queens, New York City, for over twenty-five years. From the first day of the church until now, we have been surrounded by a sea of needs. When asked, "How have you two survived?" my answer is, "We love the people and our service is an act of love for Christ. At the same time, we know we are dispensable and are intentional to put on the Oxygen Mask of Self-Care. We did not do good self-care the first eight years and almost self-destructed as a result. This journey into emotionally healthy spirituality has helped us to discover both an inward and outward balance to our life."

Pete and I are committed to the Sabbath. We take a one-day Sabbath each week; a one-month Sabbath each summer; and a three- to four-month Sabbath/sabbatical every seven years. During these Sabbath rhythms we pursue the things that give us life—hiking, music, reading, exploring new places, biking, eating at ethnic restaurants, nature, the beach, and being with our extended family and four girls.

The oxygen mask that gives you fresh air may include attending concerts, gazing at the stars through a telescope, participating in a book club, playing on a sports team, throwing clay on a pottery wheel, working with wood,

Are you pursuing those things that breathe life into you and help you to feel fully alive?

gardening, fishing, cooking, participating in extreme sports, writing poetry, making art, quilting, or simply being with friends.

The question is, "Are you pursuing those things that breathe life into you and help you to feel fully alive?" Can you cease all your work one day a week to focus on what gives you life? Consider setting aside one day when you eliminate all *shoulds* and *have to's* in order to rest and delight in God's gifts to you and around you.[3]

6. *The Mirror of Self-Confrontation*

We need this tool to protect ourselves from self-deception (Jeremiah 17:9). Placing ourselves before the Mirror of Self-Confrontation means humbly acknowledging our shortcomings and the ways in which we are responsible for our own failures and disappointments. This is what Jesus was talking about when he taught that we must take the log out of our own eye before taking the speck out of someone else's (Matthew 7:1–5).

We prefer to blame rather than take responsibility. I blamed Pete for how unhappy I was about spending summers in New York City. When I finally placed myself before the Mirror of Self-Confrontation, I realized it was easier to blame Pete than to risk making him angry by choosing to spend summers without him at my parents' beach house. Blaming him for my unhappiness allowed me to avoid facing my fear of his disapproval. At the time, it was a fear that felt worse than death.

When I finally took this log out of my own eye, I was able to exert my personal freedom to take care of my needs. I stopped blaming Pete, took responsibility for my happiness, and started spending time at my parents' home —even if my decision didn't initially meet with Pete's approval.

Self-confrontation may sound like a scary tool (and it does raise fears), but it is also a powerful tool that gives you the ability to face your own monsters head-on. It enables you to stop blaming and take back your life. In everyday life, self-confrontation may mean ...

- you stop blaming your employer for your unhappiness and begin to face your fear of looking for a different job.
- you stop complaining about your adult child's irresponsible money management and acknowledge that you do more harm than good when you keep lending him or her money.
- you stop blaming your parents for being so demanding, knowing the real issue is your inability to say no when they ask you to keep solving their problems.
- you stop blaming the church for being so demanding and contributing to your burnout. Instead, you embark on the difficult path of looking inward to

discern why you have difficulty setting appropriate, healthy boundaries.

- you stop blaming others for your poor presentation at work, admitting you were too prideful to ask for help beforehand and too afraid to invite feedback afterward.

If we fail to make good use of this tool, we will never live into the God-given freedom to choose our own lives. Pope John Paul II put it this way, "Truth and freedom either go hand in hand or together they perish in misery." We cannot achieve full personal freedom without full personal truth.

Think back over your week. Were there moments when you said something you wished you had not? Were there any behaviors or actions you regretted doing? What was going on in your heart? If you could do the week over, what might you do differently? If there is any person that you need to go back and speak to, set a note in your calendar to take that courageous step. Be careful not to beat yourself up. Offer your findings to God, trusting his promise that "if we confess our sins, he is faithful and just and will forgive us our sins and purify us from all unrighteousness" (1 John 1:9).

7. The Key of Hope

From the creation of the world God has always provided hope. It is built into the very fabric of nature's seasons as we observe the cycle of death and newness every winter and summer. The most concrete reminder of the reality that we serve a living God who longs to instill hope in his children is grounded in the life, death, burial, and resurrection of our Lord Jesus.

The golden Key of Hope unlocks this truth and releases us from the prison of living in the past. Living without hope is like trying to drive a car forward while looking only in the rearview mirror. Focusing too much on the past prevents us from looking ahead to the future.

When life becomes difficult, it is easy to become stuck in cycles of negative thinking: "I will never let that happen again," we say to ourselves. And we expend all our energy thinking about what we don't want. The Key of Hope points us to the more important question: "What do I want?" This frees us to take responsibility for a better future that, in cooperation with the Holy Spirit, we can create for ourselves. Moreover, it keeps us from getting stuck in regrets, resentments, and blaming others.

Hope opens doors that we may think are locked but are not. For example, as a pastor's spouse, there have been many times when I lost hope that we would ever have an enjoyable and sustainable life. I wrongly believed that past patterns would simply continue into the future and that there was nothing I could do about it. But that was not true. The gospel offers hope not just for heaven but for this life, here and now. No matter how difficult the past may be, it doesn't mean a better future is impossible.

- Perhaps your family did not know how to express difficult emotions. You can learn.
- You don't know how to build trust with people. You can learn.

- You don't know how to have intimate relationships. You can learn.
- You don't know how to use your voice to assert yourself in an honest, direct, respectful way. You can learn.
- You are scared to death of self-confrontation. You can learn to do it and not only survive, but thrive.
- You avoid conflict at all costs. You can learn to confront it without fear.
- You can pursue a desirable future, getting the necessary training you need to make healthy changes in your life. You can learn.

Christ invites us to place our hope in his power to redeem even the most difficult circumstances, and he invites us to participate with him in creating a positive future. The past does not have to be the future.

What doors do you believe to be closed today? How might you insert the Key of Hope into that situation to start moving out of the past into a better future? And who might be a mature person whom you can approach in order to share your perspective and encourage you with loving, honest feedback?

The past does not have to be the future.

8. The Hat of Wisdom

God gives us the ability to live wisely and not foolishly. The entire book of Proverbs extends God's invitation to us to put on the Hat of Wisdom. God invites us to search for insight and understanding as if searching for hidden treasure (Proverbs 2:3–4). Although wisdom involves many things, I want to focus on the vital importance of the wisdom we put into practice when we think ahead and make informed decisions by anticipating potential consequences.

The wisdom of anticipating consequences requires careful thinking about short- and long-range decisions. In other words, we don't go blindly into things or make impulsive decisions. Scripture calls this quality prudence. "The simple believe anything, but the prudent give thought to their steps" (Proverbs 14:15). This applies to all kinds of decisions, whether buying a used car, pursuing a relationship, making a career change, agreeing to a new commitment, accumulating credit card debt, or buying something we don't need that happens to be on sale. You enthusiastically purchase a used car because it was the right price. Within one month the car breaks down and needs costly repairs. Now you realize you should have brought it to a car mechanic to assess it before buying it. When we practice such prudence and foresight, we take responsibility for our lives and futures.

In the early years of our ministry, we rapidly expanded the church by adding more services and planting new churches. We didn't think through the implications of this expansion on staff marriages, our personal relationships with God, or our capacity to provide pastoral care to so many additional people. As a result, we made promises we couldn't keep and then made more unwise and quick decisions out of fear and anxiety. Had we slowed down and anticipated the potential consequences of our decisions, we might have avoided a great deal of hardship and disappointment.

Many people avoid thinking too much about the potential consequences of a decision out of fear about what they may discover. For example, you decide to leave your current job for another that offers more money. But you didn't anticipate the long, difficult commute, rising gas prices, longer hours, and the expense of new clothes appropriate for this new position. After a few months you realize you are now taking home less money than your previous job. In hindsight, you may say, "If I had only thought of that before!" or "It seemed like such a good idea at the time."

The Hat of Wisdom gives us the right and the responsibility to pause, gather information, and then to evaluate what we know about an issue. It requires us to think critically before making decisions, recognizing that giving thought to our ways is both a privilege and a gift from God.

Identify a poor decision you made in the past. What do you wish you had done differently? What do you regret? What do you now realize? How can you apply those lessons to a current situation you are facing today?

9. *The Badge of Courage*

The Badge of Courage enables us to take healthy risks. This tool is powerful because it is forged in flames of God's love for us. We can be courageous because we don't have to prove our worth to earn God's love. As a result, we can take risks and do the sometimes uncomfortable and difficult things required to grow up into emotionally and spiritually mature adults.

Taking hold of personal freedom requires courage

and faith. There are no guarantees that things will not get harder before they get better. You can expect resistance when you begin to challenge unhealthy patterns and shed your false self. You are entering a fiery furnace that will burn out of you all that is inauthentic, illusionary, and pretentious. Choosing an authentic life does not mean choosing an easy life; these decisions are difficult and involve pain. The question is whether the pain you choose will be redemptive or destructive. Redemptive pain demands that you die to the right things so you can move closer to your destiny. Destructive pain never leads to anything but more pain; it simply recycles the same problems over and over.

Putting on the Badge of Courage enables you to consider all the tools in the Personal Freedom Toolkit. Take the Badge of Courage and look back over each tool, reflecting on the following questions:

- *Fence of Separateness*: Where do you allow your boundaries to be crossed?
- *The Voice of Declaration*: When do you have difficulty speaking up?
- *The Yes/No Medallion*: To whom do you find it difficult to say no?
- *The Heart of Feelings*: Which feelings do you avoid?
- *The Oxygen Mask of Self-Care*: Where are you failing in self-care?
- *Mirror of Self-Confrontation*: Where are you skimming on truth?
- *The Key of Hope*: In what area of your life do you think things will never change?

- *The Hat of Wisdom*: In what area of your life are you being impulsive and not asking difficult questions?
- *The Badge of Courage*: For which one of these tools do you need the most courage?

When we quit blaming and utilize our God-given personal freedom, our sense of helplessness evaporates. We realize we are not responsible for other people's choices; they are. We can't change others, but we can change ourselves—with God's grace.

This leads to the question of how we care about others and serve them while at the same time allowing them to mature and take responsibility for their own burdens (see Galatians 6:2, 4). We will address this challenging question in our next chapter—to quit overfunctioning.

6

Quit Overfunctioning

We overfunction when we do for others what they can and should do for themselves. Overfunctioners prevent people, including themselves, from growing up. The street, however, runs both ways. Wherever you find an overfunctioner, an underfunctioner inevitably follows close behind. Overfunctioning dangerously imperils friendships, marriages, churches, workplaces, and families. I know this well. I was an overfunctioner for many years.

A poem entitled "Millie's Mother's Red Dress" by Carol Lynn Pearson demonstrates the toxic fallout of overfunctioning. As Millie's mother lies dying, a beautiful red dress she never wore hangs in her closet. In her last moments, she recounts her regrets and the lessons she learned too late in a conversation with her daughter.

> *Well, I always thought*
> *that a good woman never takes her turn,*
> *that she's just for doing for somebody else.*
> *Do here, do there, always keep*
> *everybody else's wants tended and make sure*

yours are at the bottom of the heap.
Maybe someday you'll get to them,
but of course you never do.
My life was like that—doing for your dad,
doing for the boys, for your sisters, for you.

"You did everything a mother could."

Oh Millie, Millie, it was no good—
for you—for him. Don't you see?
I did you the worst of wrongs.
I asked nothing—for me!

When the doctor told your father, he took
it bad—came to my bed and all but shook
the life right out of me.
"You can't die.
Do you hear? What'll become of me?"
It'll be hard, all right, when I go.
He can't even find the frying pan, you know ...

I look at how some of your brothers
treat their wives now,
and it makes me sick, 'cause it was me
that taught it to them. And they learned.
They learned that a woman doesn't
even exist except to give ...
Can't even remember once when I took
myself downtown to buy something beautiful—
for me.

Except last year when I got that red dress.

Oh, Millie—I always thought if you take
nothing for yourself in this world,

you'd have it all in the next somehow.
I don't believe that anymore.
I think the Lord wants us to have something—
here—and now …

I passed up my turn for so long
I would hardly know how to take it …

Do me the honor, Millie,
of not following in my footsteps.
Promise me that.[1]

Millie's mother realized at the end of her life that she served neither her family nor herself well. She overfunctioned at the expense of her own soul. Her family underfunctioned, stunting their growth into maturity. She did for them what they could and should have done for themselves. At the end of her life, all she had was painful regrets about the harm she had done.

Stepping Out from the Bottom of the Heap

Can you relate to Millie? I can. For years I put myself at the "bottom of the heap." I too was doing for everybody else, always putting myself last. I was the primary parent for our daughters. I took care of our home. I paid the bills. I managed our schedules. I planned yearly holidays and days off. I created special occasions for our family. I did birthdays and monitored all medical and dental appointments. I did all the cleaning, cooking, laundry, and shopping. I entertained groups from our church weekly and overnight guests monthly. I lived as if I were Superwoman, doing the work of three people.

Pete was an underfunctioner at home because he was an overfunctioner at work. He did the job of three people at our church. He lived as if he were Superman. This created large gaps at home that I filled. In fact, my overfunctioning at home made it possible for Pete to overfunction at church. I ended up doing for Pete, as well as our daughters, many things they could and should have been doing for themselves.

I grew tired, weary, and resentful. This leaked out in sarcasm and complaining. That didn't change our situation very much. Pete may have taken the kids to an after-school soccer game, but he was still on the phone. As I began my journey into emotionally healthy spirituality, I realized I was the problem, not Pete. If I wanted Pete to stop underfunctioning at home, I needed to stop overfunctioning. I could no longer shield Pete from the consequences of his underfunctioning as a husband, as a father, and as a member of our family. If Pete didn't step up, then perhaps our daughter would not play in the local soccer league. If Pete didn't want to prepare a guest room, then there wouldn't be anymore overnight guests.

We overfunction when we do for others what they can do for themselves.

I discovered everyone in my family could each do their own laundry, including Pete. I also realized I wanted to renegotiate expectations around parenting. I did not want to be the primary parent. I wanted Pete to share an equal burden in carrying the anxiety and weight of our children's needs—emotionally, academically, physically, and spiritually. I also did not want to cook seven nights a week. Pete was capable of learning how to prepare food and taking responsibility for dinner two nights a week. And it wasn't all smooth sailing. I can assure you, my family— especially my Italian-American mother-in-law—was not cheering me from the sidelines.

Pete was forced to face his own overfunctioning role at church and underfunctioning role at home. He wasn't happy about it—at least at first, especially when it came to cooking and laundry. Over time, however, he learned a few things. In the short term, the quality of our meals declined significantly. I didn't mind as long as there was food on the table at 6:00 p.m. and I didn't have to think about how it got there.

Pete was less upset with the changes than our daughters. Their anxiety came out as anger. "Mothers are supposed to do the cooking. You're mean!" yelled Faith. Eva complained, "Dad's cooking is horrible. I'm starving to death." She was right about Pete's cooking; he had a lot to learn. But I remained resolute and calm, determined to achieve some balance in my life.

Despite some initial resentment, Pete came to realize how much he loved co-parenting. In the beginning of taking on more responsibilities at home, Pete continued to do the jobs of three people at church. But now he was dropping a lot of balls at work. He soon realized how much he was overworking at the church.

Pete changed the way he functioned at church. He could no longer launch new initiatives without taking into account his responsibilities at home. He slowed down the church, eliminating, for example, large events and outreaches that absorbed enormous energy and time. God-given limits and boundaries became part of his vocabulary.

Pete reordered his priorities at church and learned to say no to events that impacted his new commitments to our marriage and family, even if it disappointed some people. Interestingly, the church grew and flourished as he made these changes.

Overfunctioning Inventory

Let me repeat: Overfunctioning is doing for others what they can and should do for themselves. Overfunctioning is more than simply a bad habit; it is a weed whose deep roots can often be traced back through generations in your family of origin. And the thorny branches of that weed reach far out into our workplaces, parenting, marriages, churches, and friendships.

Overfunctioning is not an all-or-nothing kind of condition; it exists on a continuum that ranges from mild to severe. Use the simple assessment below to get an idea of where you fall on the continuum. Place a checkmark in the boxes next to the statements that describe you.

- ☐ I generally know the right way to do things.
- ☐ I move in quickly to advise or fix things lest they fall apart.
- ☐ I have difficulty allowing others to struggle with their own problems.
- ☐ In the long run, it is simply easier to do things myself.
- ☐ I don't trust others to do as good a job as I can.
- ☐ I often do what is asked of me, even if I am already overloaded.

☐ I don't like to rock the boat, so I cover for others' shortcomings.

☐ Other people describe me as "stable" and as always "having it together."

☐ I don't like asking for help because I don't want to be a burden.

☐ I like to be needed.

If you checked three or more boxes, you may be over-functioning; if you checked four to seven boxes, you probably have a moderate case of overfunctioning; if you scored eight or above, you are in trouble!

The Five Deadly Consequences of Overfunctioning

It's easy, and perhaps tempting, to discount the damage done to ourselves and others because of overfunctioning, but it's no small matter. There are at least five deadly consequences of this behavior: it breeds resentment, perpetuates immaturity, prevents us from focusing on our life's calling, erodes our spiritual life, and destroys community.[2]

Overfunctioning Breeds Resentment

Perhaps you recall the story of Mary and Martha from Luke 10. Martha, in classic overfunctioning mode, is completely caught up in the demands of preparing an important meal for some very distinguished guests: Jesus and his twelve disciples. Among other things, her to-do list includes harvesting or shopping for ingredients; setting a large table; prepping food; borrowing mats, tables, and serving plates from the neighbors; cleaning the house; hiring a musician for the right background music; serving the meal; cleaning up the meal; and, perhaps most importantly, making sure that everything goes perfectly. But even when preparations seem to be going well, Martha is angry and resentful—especially at her sister Mary, who sits enjoying the company of Jesus. Martha is too angry to enjoy Jesus herself.

Martha's overfunctioning is cloaked in the guise of caring for the needs of others. However, in trying to accomplish too much, she not only loses sight of herself but of the very purpose of all her hard work—to welcome and care for her guests, including Christ himself. Martha confuses *caring about* someone with having to *take care* of them.

I relate to Martha, more than I want to admit. For most of my Christian life, what I misunderstood as caring was actually taking more responsibility for people than God was asking me to. This included everything from babysitting people's children and providing transportation to giving away money, offering my teenage children advice when they weren't asking for it, ironing Pete's shirts when he could do it himself, and being readily available for other people's crises.

On one occasion, Pete invited two well-known Christian leaders from out of town to come to our home for lunch. As usual, I worked extremely hard to present a perfect-looking home and exhausted myself cooking an elaborate meal. Beginning two days ahead, I prepared homemade clam chowder, homemade bread with cheese, and a killer—homemade chocolate cake. And all of this was done with a baby on my hip and a toddler tugging at my leg.

Sadly, I believed that my exertions themselves meant I was caring for these people. But like Martha, I was tired, cranky, and stressed out with those around me. "I'm sick and tired of this," I complained. "Why doesn't anybody help me!"

When one of Pete's lunch guests casually remarked he wasn't hungry and nonchalantly pushed away his plate, I was devastated. "How could he not appreciate my hard work?" I protested to Pete in private.

It wasn't until years later that I began to realize I could care for people without overfunctioning. I knew I had turned a corner one evening in particular when we hosted another overnight guest. I straightened the house, but I didn't clean it immaculately. I served a simple, not elaborate, dessert. I let my kids be themselves.

After dinner, we settled down in the living room with coffee. I sat and mostly listened as our guest, a fellow pastor, poured out his heart. I remember being aware of Christ's presence. If one of the kids needed something, I let Pete jump up and get it. When the dishes piled up in the sink, I let them be. I was able to be truly present with myself, with Pete, and with our guest. I thought back to Jesus' beautiful invitation to Martha. "You are worried and upset about many things, but few things are needed—or indeed only one" (Luke 10:41–42). And I began to realize that this invitation was also for me.

Overfunctioning Perpetuates Immaturity

Moses was an overfunctioning leader who mistakenly

believed his self-sacrifice helped his people. Day and night he sat before long lines of disgruntled folks trying to settle the seemingly endless disputes that arose among them. He was so overwhelmed and exhausted that it never occurred to him there might be a better way. It took an outside person, his father-in-law, Jethro, to point out the obvious: "What you are doing is not good. You and these people who come to you will only wear yourselves out. The work is too heavy for you; you cannot handle it alone" (Exodus 18:17–18). Moses' life changed dramatically when he followed Jethro's advice and appointed judges to hear most of the disputes. Until he allowed others to take up their legitimate responsibilities, Moses himself was the largest obstacle preventing the healthy growth and maturity of his people.

But old habits die hard. Later, in Numbers 11, the Bible describes how Moses' overfunctioning gets him in trouble again when the people of Israel blame him for their unhappiness with the food rations. They didn't want to struggle with learning to trust God's promises. Instead, they demand a rescue from their pain, and Moses readily accepts the role of superhero and takes full responsibility to save them. Unfortunately, in doing so, he not only engages in self-destructive behavior but also ensures the ongoing immaturity of his people.

The question Moses needed to ask himself way back when is the same one we need to ask ourselves today. Do we really love others well when ...

- we don't require our children to consistently carry age-appropriate responsibilities in the home because

we don't want to deal with their resentment and bad
attitudes.

- we protect someone we love from feeling inadequate
  or insecure by discouraging them from taking healthy
  risks for growth and achievement.
- we fulfill all the tasks needed for a successful small
  group or ministry — prepare our home to host the
  meeting, prepare materials, lead the group, provide
  refreshments, clean up, recruit and follow up with
  newcomers, pray, meet special needs of group
  members, plan small-group outings, and train an
  apprentice — and don't encourage others to take
  responsibility.
- we allow church to become a spectator sport in which
  a few carry the weight of responsibility for the many.

The lie that overfunctioning whispers in our ears is
this: You are the only thing holding everything together.
If you stop, things will fall apart. Actually, the opposite
is true. The more we overfunction, the more others are
demotivated to make changes. If we let go of our overfunctioning ways, God's work will prosper in them, in
you, and, ultimately, in many others. If we don't, we
almost guarantee that those around us will remain in
immaturity.

If an underfunctioner is going to take responsibility,
we who overfunction must cease from saving, fixing, or
advising. Growing up in any area of life is challenging
— whether financially, spiritually, emotionally, or rela-
tionally. Few underfunctioners will make the first move
because the benefits they receive are too satisfying, at
least in the short term. Somebody else bears the weight

and responsibilities, so they don't have to. To step away from what others can and should do for themselves initially appears harsh, but it is actually a loving act.

Overfunctioning Prevents You from Focusing on Your Life's Calling

At the end of his life, Jesus said to God, "I have brought you glory on earth by finishing the work you gave me to do" (John 17:4). It is doubtful we will be able to say such a thing ourselves at the end of our lives if we are overfunctioners. God had a plan for Christ's short, earthly life, and he has a plan for your life and mine. However, if we are focused too much on others, we will be easily sidetracked and miss out on the unique calling God has for us.

When we overfunction in service to others, we often underfunction for ourselves. We lose sight of our own values, beliefs, and goals, which is precisely what happened to Moses. He became so preoccupied with the problems of his people that he lost the focus of his own life's goals.

> When we overfunction in service to others, we often underfunction for ourselves.

It is sobering to think about what might have happened to Moses and the Israelites if Moses had *not* been willing to listen to Jethro and stop overfunctioning. Sometimes, like Moses, we are too close to a person or situation to discern if our efforts to provide care are hurting or helping. Would Moses ever have fulfilled his life's calling to get the people to the Promised Land if he believed he was indispensable to settling *all* their disputes?

As a mother of four and the wife of a very active ministry leader, I find it challenging to resist the temptations of overfunctioning. Sometimes it feels as if it's easier to focus on everyone else's needs than it is to take the requisite time, space, and energy to focus on my own life's goals. I must regularly ask myself, "Am I being faithful to the life God gave me? How am I integrating my role as wife and mother with my own unique passions, talents, and limits so God's unique call on my life doesn't get swallowed up in the demands of ministry and family life?"

Pete and I have worked together for many years. I normally enjoy it, but there are times when I have to say no to one of his projects because I realize it does not align with my personal goals. In our earlier years I said yes to everything, and then I grew weary and resentful because not everything Pete believed God was calling him to do was a good fit for me.

Reflect on your life for a few moments: Are you so busy focusing on others that you've lost focus on your own needs and goals? In the midst of doing things for others—children, a spouse, friends, relatives, or coworkers—do you routinely make time to ask yourself questions such as these:

- Am I being the person I want to be in this situation?
- Am I doing for others what they could and should be doing for themselves?
- Am I living in line with my values?
- Is this the work to which God has uniquely called me?
- What do I want that I am not getting?
- What result am I getting that I do not want?
- What am I not doing that I would like to be doing?

- What am I giving that I don't want to give?
- What will I do with my time when I stop overfunctioning for others?

These are difficult and challenging questions. Each of us lives within the constraints of our marital status, family, and job responsibilities. This requires thoughtfulness and planning; conversations and consultations with others will be needed for certain decisions. For example, when I decided I wanted to read for half an hour before going to sleep several times a week, I simply carved out time and space to do so. But when I decided to go away for a three-night retreat or a weekend with friends, I consulted with Pete because it impacted him, our children, and our finances.

Nonetheless, there are things that you can change, cut out, or add in order to focus on your God-given life in a healthier way. The key is to remain focused on your own life's direction while remaining in open, clear communication with the other significant people in your life.

Overfunctioning Erodes Your Spiritual Life

By the time Martha's excessive caretaking reaches its peak, she is giving commands to Jesus: "Tell [Mary] to help me!" (Luke 10:40). Her overfunctioning not only prevents her from experiencing Christ's love, it makes her resentful. She believes she knows better than Jesus what Mary, her sister, should be doing.

Christ alone is the Savior. We are called to trust and to surrender to his love. When we cross the line and put ourselves in charge of running God's world for him, we enter into dangerous territory, into the very rebellion of our ancestors, Adam and Eve.

I know I am overfunctioning when I think I don't have time to stop and be with God. For this reason, contemplative practices such as Sabbath-keeping, silence, and solitude help me to resist this temptation. God, for example, created us to work six days and to rest one. Because of my propensity to overfunction, Sabbaths are essential for me; it's how I intentionally set aside time for God to do the work that only God can do—in me and in the world around me.

I recall how I felt one Friday afternoon especially as I prepared for a Sabbath that was to begin at 6:00 that evening. I had finished my emails, closed down my computer, folded the laundry, checked off all my errands, returned phone calls, and completed all the church work required in preparation for the following Sunday. The house was in order. As I symbolically turned off the lights on Friday evening to mark the official beginning of my Sabbath, I prayed, "Okay, God, I'm going off duty. You're in charge for the next twenty-four hours."

God invites us to take responsibility for our own lives and not be overresponsible for others.

Something inside of me shifted. I actually breathed a sigh of relief that I didn't have to do anything for the next twenty-four hours. I was really going to let God be in control of the universe. I was free.

What about you? Are you able to accept God's weekly invitation to stop and rest, knowing that he is capable of running the world without you for at least one day in seven? Or are you on the Martha plan, overfunctioning to the point that it's become damaging to your relationship with Christ? One of the great signs that you truly believe in God is when you rest in his sovereignty and saving power and resist the powerful temptation to overfunction.

God doesn't want us to overfunction or underfunction. Rather, God invites us to take responsibility for our own lives and not be overresponsible for others.

Overfunctioning Destroys Community

The stories of Moses and Martha provide clear pictures of how overfunctioning negatively impacts communities. When Moses was dealing with the food crisis described in Numbers 11, the community atmosphere became so toxic that Moses despaired of life: "If this is how you are going to treat me," Moses pleads with God, "please go ahead and kill me" (Numbers 11:15). And the situation isn't much better with Martha. Imagine you are one of the dinner guests trying to enjoy that great meal with Jesus while Martha stomps angrily around the room, muttering under her breath and staring daggers through her sister. Fun times!

If my spouse or teenager is underfunctioning and I am overfunctioning in maintaining the relationship, my actions distort God's original intention for community. When people function properly according to God's design, there is truth and relationships are marked by "love, joy, peace, forbearance, kindness, goodness, faithfulness, gentleness and self-control" (Galatians 5:22–23). When overfunctioning and underfunctioning are present, relationships are marked instead by dissension, conflict, blaming, helplessness, anger, and despair.

Author Ed Freidman describes the negative relational impact of overfunctioning this way: "When one over-functions in another's space, it can cause disintegration of the other's being."[3] I like the word *disintegration* because it refers to inhibiting the growth and maturation of a person's God-given sense of self. Overfunctioners actually believe they know what is best for everyone. In doing so, they invade and limit the development of others.

This occurs when a parent of a fourteen-year-old makes that child's decisions to protect them from the world. The parent organizes the child's free time, chooses extracurricular activities, picks out clothing, and maybe even arranges friendships. Adult children are stunted in their growth when they live at home but do not contribute emotionally or financially. Employers discourage initiative and creativity when they move in quickly to rescue employees rather than allow them to struggle with their own problems. Church leaders and members who always serve and fill in empty slots for volunteers, without sharing their own limits and weaknesses, reinforce underfunctioning in others.

Healthy community requires that individuals take responsibility appropriate to their age, life stage, gifts, and abilities. It is unlikely the underfunctioners will make the first move. For this reason, the overfunctioners have to face themselves first. Then there is the real possibility that underfunctioners will also embark on the life-changing journey of spiritual and emotional maturity.

If you are an overfunctioner, you may not be able to make the underfunctioners more responsible, but you can make yourself less responsible. Minimally, your community will function more authentically, with less frustration, exhaustion, and anger, and distancing that so often accompanies the rescuing and bailing out of others inappropriately.

Breaking Free from Overfunctioning

To quit overfunctioning is easier said than done. The patterns of relating that we create are often fixed and long-standing. We learn overfunctioning by observation and osmosis from our own family; so resistance to breaking free is profound—both from within us and without.

We tend not to see we have the problem because we are only trying to be helpful. Change can be profoundly difficult and anxiety-producing. To remain calm when you stop overfunctioning requires staying the course throughout these four phases: admit you are overfunctioning, unleash the earthquake, prepare for chaos, and stand firm. Each of these phases thrusts us into deeper levels of maturity in our relationship with God, others, and ourselves.

Admit That You Are Overfunctioning

Overfunctioning comes in many shapes and forms. It can range from sewing a button on your spouse's shirt when they can do it, to repeatedly bailing out your adult children financially. You will need to discern your own unique warning signs. One thing that tips me off that I am overfunctioning is when I begin to believe things will fall apart if I don't do what is needed.

I was a stay-at-home mom when my kids were young,

but I also worked part time out of our home during school hours. One year, however, I considered taking a job at the local YMCA working in recreation, a great love of mine. The hours, however, were 3:00 to 6:00 p.m., three days a week.

Immediately several large obstacles surfaced in my mind. How could I disturb my husband's life? He was already under a lot of pressure. Pete would have to rearrange his schedule in order to pick up our girls from school, drive them to their afterschool activities, and prepare dinner. I knew Pete could do it; I just wasn't sure he would, especially three days a week! I also expected my children would put up a fight if I disrupted their predictable afternoon routines.

All kinds of thoughts ran through my head.

- "Nobody can take care of them like me!"
- "I'll mess up Pete's life. This could put him over the edge in stress."
- "The kids will suffer. Things will become disorganized. He's late a lot. They're going to be full of anxiety."
- "Things will fall apart if I do this."

That final thought was like a bolt of lightning that brought me back to reality and helped me to recognize that I was slipping into overfunctioning. I knew then that I needed to take that job, regardless of the consequences. Pete and the girls needed to adjust. This was now my opportunity to stop underfunctioning in my own life and do something I enjoyed while simultaneously contributing to our family income.

You know you are crossing the line into overfunctioning when you hear yourself saying things like, "We won't
celebrate Christmas as a family unless I do it." "I'm the
only one who can do this right." "It is just easier if I do it
myself." "I'm afraid of their reaction if I ask them to do
more." And it is this realization that prepares you for the
next phase, to unleash an earthquake.

Unleash the Earthquake

Introducing change into a relational system is like unleash-
ing an earthquake—it knocks everyone and everything
off their feet and may even topple long-standing struc-
tures. This change is similar to reclaiming, discovering,
and living out your personal integrity. You admit you are
overfunctioning and are now ready to disrupt the status
quo. The rules of the relationship are about to change.
It is no longer business as usual. It is not telling someone
else what to do; it is telling them what *you* are going to
do or not do.

Few things arouse more anxiety than shifting the balance in a relationship. The underfunctioner experiences
increased anxiety and, often, countermoves to reestablish
the original unhealthy balance. Yet this moment offers
the greatest possibility for everyone involved to cross the
threshold into an accelerated season of emotional and
spiritual maturing in Christ.

The size of the earthquake depends on the level of
maturity of those involved, the history of the relationship,
and the willingness to avail themselves of outside help if
needed. But when you first quit overfunctioning, even in
something small, it can feel cataclysmic.

After processing my thoughts about taking the job at the YMCA, I told Pete about the job and how much I wanted to take it. I was prepared for him to say that he was not willing to disrupt his life so significantly. In that case, my backup plan was to find alternative childcare. Fortunately, however, he agreed, albeit reluctantly, to the changes the new job would require.

That evening we informed the kids about the change. They complained more than I expected. "Dad will forget to pick us up. We'll never make our soccer practices on time." Pete was known to be distractible so the kids were justifiably nervous about him.

"He's always on the phone," they complained. "Dad doesn't know how to take care of us the way you do."

I wasn't sure at that point if this was going to work, but I pushed through my doubts.

Prepare for Chaos

Whenever we differentiate and give up our old ways of behaving and living, we can always expect a reaction from those close to us. "Change back," or "Don't you dare," may be the words you hear. Chaos means the relational system is now operating in unpredictable ways. I have yet to see anyone who stops overfunctioning—who makes a change in themselves by becoming their true self in Christ—without at least one or two people around them getting upset.

When I began my job at the YMCA, I didn't know what was going to happen in our family dynamic. I prepared myself for the unknown. I knew it was important for me to tolerate the discomfort and remain present with why taking this job was important to me. My decision changed a pattern cemented in over ten years of marriage. While I knew this was a good decision, I struggled with guilt.

During the first few weeks of my new job, I was flooded with anxiety every day at 3:00, wondering, "Did Pete remember to pick the kids up?" I imagined them stranded alone in the schoolyard. "What was I thinking?" I berated myself. "This was a bad idea." My stomach knotted. My mind raced through a hundred unthinkable scenarios.

Then I calmed down and reminded myself that the school wouldn't let a six- and nine-year-old out alone on a New York City street. The school would call Pete and he would come. He did forget a couple of times. The kids sat in the principal's office waiting. He had to deal with their anger. Then he had scheduling conflicts because of work. He asked me to fill in. I declined. Our agreement was that he would find his own replacement if he had a schedule conflict. It was hard to not solve the problem for him.

It was also not unusual for Pete to forget that he was in charge of dinner. More than once I came home in those first few months to a house of hungry, upset children. "We don't like Dad being in charge," they cried. "Mom, you have to quit work and come home again." I let them express their feelings, but I didn't quit my job. I assured them this decision was in the best interest of us all, at least in the long run.

I stayed the course. They soon adjusted beautifully.

Stand Firm

Entrenched relational patterns are strong. You can expect

to encounter resistance when you choose to stop over-functioning. The goal of this phase is to stand firm in your decision; others are unaccustomed to seeing you in your new role. The awkwardness extends to everyone around you. Allow time for people's perceptions of both you and others to change.

For example, before I took the job, I saw myself as indispensable. As time progressed, it became evident I was not. The kids didn't need me all the time. They soon realized, "Wow, Mom has her own life apart from us!" One of my daughters remarked casually, "Gee, who would have ever thought Dad could run the house so well."

Slowly, our family settled into new rhythms. Pete came to enjoy the new experiences he had spending afternoons with our girls. Without interference from me, he discovered that he had his own unique parenting style. This marked the beginning of a move to co-parent our children. Surprising as it was to me, Pete loved it.

Our daughters also benefited from spending more time with Pete. In fact, over time, they came to enjoy his parenting style more than mine. They find his easygoing, more flexible style a pleasure. Now they say, "When are you going away, Mom?"

I too learned to relax and enjoy our new rhythm. I actually loved being dispensable. My family didn't need me to hold them together. I appreciated what the girls were receiving emotionally, mentally, physically, and spiritually as a result of being with Pete. Cooking never became his forte, but I didn't care as long as I didn't have to cook on those nights.

Navigating this change provided a kind of template for

many other changes in our future. We have learned to operate as a team with flexible roles that don't become frozen in time. We discuss and agree on changes.

I am convinced that if I keep someone from growing up by my overfunctioning, I hurt them. To love and serve others well for Christ's sake demands we discern if we are doing something they can and should be doing for themselves. Our own fears and anxieties strongly pull us to change back, especially in the face of resistance. Yet it is critical to give people time to absorb the changes going on around them. We may want to do something, not because it is best, but simply because we lack the maturity to sit back and wait.

Choose one area of your life where you are overfunctioning; it could be work, marriage, friendship, parenting, church, school. Take a few minutes to review the four phases:

- admit you are overfunctioning
- unleash the earthquake
- prepare for chaos
- stand firm

What might be a practical next step for you today? Offer this to God, asking the Holy Spirit for counsel and courage. Consider talking with a trusted mentor or mature friend. Then step forward into what God reveals to you.

When you are willing to quit overfunctioning, you open the door to the next "I Quit"—quit faulty thinking. In this next chapter, we explore the far-reaching implications of what it means to stop believing something is true when it is false. As we will see, to quit faulty thinking leads us to explore the blockages deep beneath the icebergs in our lives that hinder us from experiencing greater freedom in Christ.

7

Quit Faulty Thinking

Six hundred years ago, people believed the earth was flat. They were afraid to venture far out into the ocean out of fear they might fall off the earth.

For two thousand years, a process called "blood-letting," the withdrawal of large amounts of blood, was used to treat almost every disease—from cancer to indigestion to pneumonia.

For much of United States' history, Native Americans and African Americans were considered inferior, second-class citizens.

Less than one hundred years ago, women were denied the right to vote. Intellectual activity for women was considered injurious to their "delicate" female biology.

Faulty thinking is a deadly threat to emotional and spiritual health.

As recently as 1900, at least 99 percent of the population believed that "humans will never fly." Even in 1960 most people believed a person would never walk on the moon.

You probably know what I'm going to say next. All of

these assumptions were wrong, dead wrong. At the very least, wrong beliefs severely limit our ability to experience life and move forward into the future as God intends; at worst, faulty thinking destroys lives and civilizations.

Faulty thinking is when we believe something to be true that is false. As Mark Twain once said, "It isn't what you don't know that hurts you; it is what you know that isn't so."

Faulty thinking is a deadly threat to emotional and spiritual health. It can ...

- mire you in powerlessness
- paralyze you in hopelessness
- fill you with false guilt
- cut you off from joyful living
- obscure your hope for the future
- diminish your capacity for genuine relationships
- lock you up in unnecessary pain
- limit your God-given potential in Christ

It's also contagious and can spread. This makes faulty thinking even more dangerous because it operates, for the most part, beyond our conscious awareness. Eradicating this deadly disease requires such radical surgery that it can almost be compared to getting a brain transplant!

My Long Journey out of Faulty Thinking

When Pete and I started our church, we both suffered from acute cases of faulty thinking in several areas, including marriage, parenting, ministry, and spirituality.

Our understanding of Christian community is one area in particular that was caught in the clutches of faulty thinking. When we started our church, it included several young families. To combat the loneliness and lack of connection that plagues large urban centers like New York, we all moved into the same neighborhood in order to be intentional about forming a community. In fact, we not only lived in the same neighborhood but in houses attached to one another.

Pete and I owned a "railroad apartment," which means the rooms were consecutive from the front to the back of the house. In other words, there were no separate hallways; you had to go through one room to get to the next. Since our bedroom also served as the hallway into the backyard, hosting church cookouts required people to parade through our bedroom to get to the backyard. This did not excite me, but I put up with it for the sake of community.

We had many fun and meaningful experiences together in those early years as God began to birth something new and exciting. We sought to spend our free time together, raise our kids together, and share goals together. This meant a lot of togetherness—a lot.

As a community, however, we were crippled by three major factors. The *first* was that we didn't know how to respect each other's differences. For years I felt guilty over my need for beauty and space. When we moved eight years later, I felt at fault for wanting to move from our small apartment to a single-family home in a different neighborhood in Queens. The irony is that I myself judged another family when they chose to relocate to a suburban, easier place to live. Not only did we not understand healthy separateness and togetherness, we also did not have a lot of room for complexity, ambiguity, and questions.

Our *second* major problem was the belief that intimate friendships not only could but *should always* be with people in your church. Churches provide a lovely context for close friendships, but that is very different than the faulty belief that a healthy church community *always* equals close friendships. Churches as communities serve many purposes. We have a common mission, common values, and a common worship—to name a few. For some, the church community will be a primary source of close friendships. For others, it is not.

Because of our faulty belief that community equaled intimate friendship, Pete and I became close friends with the same people we employed, mentored, counseled, and led spiritually. He was the senior pastor and spiritual leader of our church. At times, he was also the supervisor and boss of more than one of our friends. And I was often a team leader and mentor of these same friends.

Problems arose when we needed to separate our informal friendships from these other more formal roles. Inevitably, the friendship—for us or for our friends—was negatively impacted. Relationships were strained and hurt feelings often followed.

It took many years, along with a few wise mentors, to uncover the faulty thinking that genuine community *always* equals close friendships. What we learned is that it is more accurate to state that close friendships do develop in healthy churches and community; that is to be celebrated and encouraged. The problem comes with the word *always*.

I am much more aware of the fragility and danger of dual roles now, especially when one holds a significant leadership role within a church setting. In a dual role, I am both an employer and a friend or both your pastor and your friend. Dual roles aren't automatically wrong or inappropriate, though sometimes they can be, but they are complex and require great maturity from both people in order to navigate them well.[1]

Our *third* major problem was believing we could live in healthy, close, Christian community without learning key emotionally healthy skills such as listening maturely, speaking honestly, and resolving conflict. We did not have the ability to deal with marital conflicts that spilled over into other contexts, outbursts of anger or frustration in awkward settings, unspoken resentments, and differing expectations. We didn't know ourselves well. How were we going to share appropriately with one another?

I highlighted a few areas of my own faulty thinking around community, but there are innumerable ways we engage in faulty thinking in our lives. Each one has vast implications and consequences on how we live out our faith in Jesus Christ—in the workplace, our families, and the church.

Three Types of Faulty Thinking

In his book *Hand-Me-Down Blues*, psychologist Michael Yapko summarizes three major types of faulty thinking that distort the way we see life:

1. All-or-Nothing Thinking
2. Taking Things Personally
3. Thinking Things Will Never Change

All three of these played a part in the confusion and pain I experienced in building community at New Life. Yet their applications, as we will see, extend into every area of our lives.

These distortions are rarely talked about in our churches or addressed in spiritual formation or discipleship training. But when we choose to quit these few simple but destructive distortions, we get unstuck from powerlessness, hopelessness, false guilt, and unnecessary pain. We experience God's promise: "For the Spirit God gave us does not make us timid, but gives us power, love and self-discipline" (2 Timothy 1:7). With these tools we are empowered to move into the future God has for us.

Faulty Thinking 1: All-or-Nothing Thinking

All-or-nothing thinking exaggerates; it makes things much bigger than they are. When one aspect of life does not go well, all-or-nothing thinking globalizes the experience so it characterizes everything in our lives. All-or-nothing thinking interprets events and circumstances in black and white. There is little room for the gray in life, for nuances, for making the fine distinctions that are so much a part of our lives. All-or-nothing thinking sees the forest but not the trees. For example:

- A job interview doesn't go well and you think, "I'm such a loser."
- A bad experience with one person who claims to be

a Christian leads you to conclude that all Christians
are hypocrites.

- You get a B on an exam and decide you are a failure.
- You buy a car that is a lemon and conclude, "I'll never find a good car."
- Your patience wears thin after a long week and you think, "I'm a horrible parent because I screamed at my kids."
- The discussion in last night's small-group meeting was stilted and awkward. You conclude, "I'm a bad leader because we didn't have a good discussion last night."
- After planning a special date for you and your spouse, a rude and inept waiter ruins your meal so that all you can think is, "Our whole evening is shot!"

We observe the biblical character Jacob suffering from a classic case of all-or-nothing thinking when he cries out, "Joseph is no more and Simeon is no more, and now you want to take Benjamin. Everything is against me!" (Genesis 42:36). Good things were happening in Jacob's life, but he could not see them. When this one thing appeared to go wrong, *everything*, for Jacob, was awful. He wrongly believed his son, Joseph, was dead. And now he believed two more sons were going to be lost.

His concern was valid. Yet his global thinking that "everything is against me" was not true. He failed to see the many ways God had blessed him and was about to greatly bless him. He failed to discern that God was working out a larger, long-range plan of saving his family from starvation by moving them to Egypt. In time, their family would form the foundation of the nation of Israel, out of which the salvation of the world would come forth.

Our all-or-nothing thinking is a tragedy. We believe something that is untrue and then spread that to others around us. This is where my all-or-nothing thinking about community led me. I wrongly believed biblical community could only look one way. I convinced myself I did not have choices and became overwhelmed. Consequently, I found myself in a low-level depression born out of a sense of powerlessness and hopelessness.

Consider the following examples of what it looks like to correct a distortion:

Faulty Thinking	Accurate Thinking
My boss will never change.	If God can change me, God can change my boss. I can also develop new strategies for relating to my boss that may help our relationship.
The whole church service was ruined today when that cell phone went off during the message.	I felt irritated when that cell phone went off, but there were so many other great parts to the service — worship, the message, the fellowship afterward.
Men can't be trusted.	I was once betrayed by a man, but I know other men who are faithful and trustworthy.
I'm a loser because he broke up with me.	I have learned some helpful things from the painful end of this relationship. And I am successful in other areas of my life — fitness, work, relationships with my family, and my spiritual life.

Faulty Thinking	Accurate Thinking
Lawyers are deceitful.	There are some dishonest lawyers and some really great ones.
She complains about everything.	She has areas of her life that are difficult, but she doesn't complain about her job, her appearance, or her parents.
I feel totally stressed out.	I am stressed out about the possibility of not passing an exam at school. But many other areas of my life are not stressed out— my relationships, my church, my finances, my good health.

When our statements include words like *always, all, everybody,* or *never,* these are usually tip-offs that we are engaging in faulty thinking. A simple change in wording can create a major change in us and enable us to reframe a situation differently.

When we engage in all-or-nothing thinking, we easily miss the ways God shows up in our lives. Nathanael, when he heard the Messiah was from the small town of Nazareth, replied: "Nazareth! Can anything good come from there?" (John 1:46). He made a wrong judgment based on a stereotype. Jesus didn't take it personally or get defensive. Instead he corrected Nathanael's imma-ture distortion and invited him to follow him and have his eyes opened to many greater things in the future.

> *When we engage in all-or-nothing thinking, we easily miss the ways God shows up in our lives.*

Faulty Thinking 2: Taking Things Personally

We take things personally when we take offense at or take responsibility or blame for something before we have all the data. We are prone to ignore the ambiguity of most situations and rush too quickly to a negative interpretation of events. However, in the vast majority of cases, our interpretation is not based on reality but on stories we tell ourselves. For example:

- A friend is late for our lunch appointment. She doesn't respect me.
- I didn't get a raise this year. They must believe I am doing a poor job.
- I wasn't asked to be in leadership. The pastor must believe I don't have the gifts.
- I didn't get the job I so desperately wanted. I must be a poor interviewer.
- My name was not in the credits for the Christmas production. They must have felt my contribution was not important.

When we land on a negative interpretation because we don't have all the data, we bring down upon ourselves much unnecessary grief. This wrecks havoc in our relationships, leaving us victims or irresponsible blamers. It is easy to accumulate a bag full of resentments that are based on something untrue.

I remember one incident when I was upset and hurt because I did not get invited out to dinner but heard "a whole group of friends went." I took it personally, telling myself that they really didn't care about me. Actually, it was a spontaneous lunch that simply happened after I had left for the day. There weren't any formal invitations beyond, "Hey, let's go for lunch." I was offended by something that was an illusion. I wasted energy ruminating over something that wasn't even true.

The ninth commandment states: "You shall not give false testimony against your neighbor" (Exodus 20:16). Yet we break this commandment when we jump to conclusions about other people that likely are not true. Our resentments often then turn to guilt for our inability to forgive them. And we wonder why so much of our spirituality and community life is so complicated and messy!

In any given situation, there are many possible reasons for why things happen the way they do—and there's a good chance that none of them is about you! Consider some examples on the chart below.

Faulty Thinking	Accurate Thinking
He did not return my phone call or email. He must be upset with me.	He may not have gotten the messages. He may have been in a rush and didn't have the time. He may have forgotten or been distracted by other concerns.
I was not invited out to the group lunch at work. They don't like me.	Maybe they had to have a working lunch around their project. Perhaps they have their reasons for not inviting me and that is okay. They are free to choose.
John didn't acknowledge me at church today. He is avoiding me.	John may have been distracted or focused on something else and didn't see me.

Faulty Thinking	Accurate Thinking
I did not get the job. I don't have the ability to get a job in today's market.	I didn't get this particular job. Since the boss's nephew interviewed too, he probably did get the job. I can get the training/coaching I need to get a job in today's market.
Susan was silent in the small group that I lead. I don't think she likes my leadership.	Susan may be very tired or be concerned about a difficulty she's not yet ready to talk about.

Much of life is ambiguous and open to interpretation. When we make quick, impulsive judgments, they are often wrong.

Mary, Jesus' mother, is a remarkable example of someone who did not take things personally. It is quite moving to ponder her apparent lack of resentment toward Joseph after he planned to divorce her quietly. As far as we know, she had no nasty words for the innkeeper who wouldn't give her a room even though she was nine months pregnant. Later, when it came time to consecrate the baby Jesus in the temple, Simeon informed her that "a sword will pierce your own soul too" (Luke 2:35). Rather than be offended or resentful toward this old man's difficult words, as any protective parent might be, the Bible says that Mary pondered and treasured these things in her heart (Luke 2:48–51).

We don't know what Mary was thinking, but she could easily have convinced herself: "There must be something wrong with me," or "There must be something wrong with these people around me." She appears to demonstrate great restraint in not telling herself negative stories about others when she did not understand their actions. Her ability not to take things personally is, perhaps, one of the great secrets of her spirituality.

Her relationship with God apparently protected her heart from labeling others as "bad" or "evil" for the ways they treated or spoke to her. She did not retaliate when she was misunderstood. We don't observe Mary drinking the spiritual poison of misinterpreting the actions of others. In the same way, when we don't take things personally, it is both a path to and a sign of a genuine spirituality.

Faulty Thinking 3: Thinking Things Will Never Change

This damaging line of thinking relates to your view of the future. If you believe things will never change, you remain deeply rooted in the past. When you assume that you, others, or a situation can change, you have the energy to apply yourself to make changes.

Consider how your family of origin approached challenging situations and difficulties. It is likely that you handle them in a similar fashion. When we engage in the faulty thinking that things will never change, we think things like this:

- I'll never have a great relationship.
- Our family will always be dysfunctional.
- I'll never be happy as long as I'm single.
- We'll never find a great teacher like we had in Pastor Smith.
- I'll never be happy in this family.
- Our child will always be difficult.

• I'll never have any friends.

King Saul and his army believed things would never change—they would always be incapable of defeating the mighty Goliath and the Philistine army. They were wrong. God used David, a young shepherd boy, with a godly perspective and a new strategy to change things. The apostle Peter believed things would never change. As a Jewish believer, he never entered the home of a Gentile. He had a faulty belief that Jews and Gentiles should remain separate as the church began to grow. Through a vision, however, God showed Peter that this could change (Acts 10–11).The disciples believed things would never change after Jesus was crucified and buried. They were wrong. Jesus rose from the dead and sent the Holy Spirit at Pentecost to birth a global, international church numbering in the tens of millions.

The past does not have to predict the future. Things can change for the better. The future does not have to hold more of the same. We can change. Consider the examples on the chart below.

Faulty Thinking	Accurate Thinking
I'll never have a healthy relationship with the opposite sex.	I can learn the skills needed for successful relationships with the opposite sex. My past doesn't have to be my future.
My boss will never understand me.	I can try approaching my boss in different ways. The past doesn't have to be the future.

Faulty Thinking	Accurate Thinking
Our marriage will always be hard.	I can get the necessary help and coaching so my marriage becomes a pleasure. The past doesn't have to be the future.
My son will always be difficult because of his learning disability.	I can learn ways to better deal with my son's difficulties that can improve our relationship. The future doesn't have to be like the past.
We'll never find a home we like and can afford.	With time, patience, good stewardship, and prayer, we can find a home, perhaps even in a different location, or we can adjust our requirements. Our future is not limited to our past experience in searching for a home.

For years I feared our church would never change. Conflicts and crisis, I believed, would always negatively impact the quality of our lives. Even today I sometimes have a visceral reaction when I hear there is "trouble at church." God did not take me out of my church, but he did change me, and our church, into greater wholeness and holiness. I learned, and continue to learn, to overcome the faulty thinking that things will never change.

Your future can be better than anything you experienced before. The future doesn't have to be more of the same past, hurtful patterns. Take the energy you have invested in needlessly overthinking the past and put it into making changes for the future.

Busting through the Wall of Faulty Thinking

Quitting faulty thinking demands the best of you. I describe this as "busting through the wall" because it is such a challenging, counterintuitive skill. It is only in the last few years that I began to focus, as part of my formation in Christ, on faulty thinking. In doing so, three key principles have emerged to form the foundation around which I have busted through this particular wall:

1. Know when *not* to follow your feelings.
2. Stop mind reading.
3. Do something different.

For long-term breakthrough in this area, whether it is with a coworker, a friend, a spouse, a parent, or a child, you must engage all three practices.

Know When Not to Follow Your Feelings

As we noted in chapter 3, Scripture reveals God as an emotional being who feels; God is a person. Having been created in his image, we too have the ability to experience emotions. Learning to listen to my feelings and to follow them—when appropriate—revolutionized my life in Christ and ultimately helped me to discover the "Quits" in this book. However, there is a time and place not to follow our feelings because they can mislead us. Consider a few examples.

A friend does not return your email or phone call for three days. You feel awful, wondering what you did or said to possibly offend her. It feels similar to how your mother withdrew from you growing up when you did something wrong. You sleep poorly, mulling over negative scenarios.

You are in a meeting at work and someone aggressively disagrees with the facilitator of the meeting. You become nervous and want to run out as tension fills the room. You are unable to participate in the rest of the meeting. It feels similar to the unresolved tension at your dinner table between your parents when you were a child.

Your husband says he will be home by 7:00 p.m. but doesn't arrive until 7:30. You are so upset that you go upstairs to your room and do not eat dinner with him. His apology and explanations mean nothing. You feel devalued and wonder if you can remain married to such an insensitive person. It feels similar to the anxiety you had as a child in depending on your father, who was often late and rarely got you to places on time.

A person in your small group talks incessantly, crippling the group dynamics. You are the facilitator and know it is your responsibility to deal with this person. You don't sleep at night, imagining innumerable bad scenarios if you should do so. You feel powerless, which is similar to how you felt growing up when you were forbidden to speak up in your home.

Your employee has handed in a report with errors and discrepancies. You are afraid of how he might react if you ask him about it. You follow your feelings and avoid him for the next two weeks. You are reminded of your brother's explosive temper tantrums whenever your parents would question him about his behavior.

In all of these scenarios, the problem arises when feelings from the past hijack clear thinking in the present.

The present situation feels familiar to something from the past and triggers a disproportionate response. Our feelings have been so hardwired that they override our logical thought process. Suddenly, we find ourselves over-reacting. Overwhelming feelings prevent us from asking clarifying questions: What is going on here? What are the facts? What do I know to be true? What outcome do I want? Are my feelings relevant to this situation, or should I set them aside in this case?

God has given us an inner guidance system to move through life—thinking and feeling. It is essential that we pay attention to our feelings. But then we must think about what to do with them. Knowing when to follow our feelings and when *not* to is indispensable if we are to grow up into spiritual adulthood in Christ.

Stop Mind Reading[2]

God is omniscient—he knows all things about all situations. And God alone knows what is going on in the minds of other people. Yet, we routinely play God when we make assumptions about another person or interpret a certain behavior without verifying the facts. These assumptions unleash much needless pain and confusion. In fact, the application of this one simple skill holds within it the key to preventing large-scale faulty thinking in your family, workplace, and church.

Imagine your husband, who usually calls you while at work, doesn't call one day. You begin to wonder if he is angry with you. You did have an argument last night, but you thought it got resolved. You assume the worst. All day long you stew over his apparent immature behavior. How dare he give you the cold shoulder!

You choose to ignore him when he arrives home and go to bed without saying good night. He remains at the kitchen table doing paperwork, not asking if anything is wrong. This confirms your hypothesis about his immaturity. Things are even worse than you thought.

"Who knows what tomorrow will bring?" you mutter to yourself in resignation as you turn off the light.

The truth, you learn later, is that he did not call because of an emergency at work. Yet you created an intricate scenario in your mind that was not true.

Imagine you are part of a church ministry team planning a big event. As director, you are exchanging quite a few emails with the rest of the team. You notice that one of the team members, Ken, who used to be warm and friendly, now shoots back terse replies. You interpret this as passive-aggressive behavior and assume he must be upset with you for something. Two can play at that game, so you fire off a few short, curt emails in return. Soon thereafter, you speak to Ken on the phone.

We routinely play God when we make assumptions about another person.

He is warm and engaging. You realize you wrongly "read his mind" in interpreting his emails negatively. You caused yourself unnecessary angst and murdered him in your heart.

In both scenarios, you spiral downward by negatively interpreting the behavior of another and making assumptions about what they're thinking. These turn into hidden landmines in relationships. Slowly, you build up resentments. You hurt yourself. You build invisible walls to keep others out. And worst of all, you quench God's Spirit within you.

Think of a person with whom you might be mind reading or about whom you are making assumptions you have not verified. At an appropriate time, ask them the following question: "May I have permission to read your mind?" or, "Can I check out an assumption I have?" or, "Do I have permission to check out my thinking with you?"[3]

Once they say yes, consider the examples below for ways to check out your thinking and stop the mind reading ...

- "I think that you think I'm responsible for the Christmas shopping this year. Is that correct?"
- "I'm wondering if you think that I think you are a bad person for not remembering my birthday. Is that correct?"
- "I noticed that you didn't return my phone calls for a few days. That's unusual for you, so I'm wondering if there is something wrong."
- "I'm puzzled that you gave Jane and Richard big hugs but passed me over. I'm wondering if I said or did something to upset you."
- "I noticed you didn't call me from work today. Is everything all right, or is there still some lingering tension after our disagreement last night?"

The stories we tell ourselves have an enormous impact on our feelings. Consider the difference of what goes on in your mind when a friend, who agrees to meet you for dinner, is forty minutes late. How different are your feelings when you tell yourself, "Maybe he had an accident driving here," or "This relationship is clearly more important to me than it is to him!" Each interpretation generates a different feeling. Why? Because our feelings are closely related to the story we tell ourselves about the things going on around us.

To quit faulty thinking and maintain good emotional and spiritual health, we must make an intentional decision to stop mind reading and to verify our assumptions by talking to people—*in person* instead of in our heads.

Do Something Different

You may be familiar with Albert Einstein's oft-quoted definition of insanity: "Doing the same thing over and over again and expecting different results." Year after year I did the same thing over and over again; yet I complained that nothing was changing. Life, I assumed, would always be hard. I said yes to everyone and everything because I wanted people to think I was superwoman. I blamed Pete for my unhappiness. I put on my happy face for others. I denied my sadness, anger, and fear. I put myself last, ignoring things that brought me life and joy.

What will you regret twenty years from now if you don't do something to change your situation?

In order to break free from the deadly clutches of faulty thinking, I had to do something different.

For years, I had a mantra playing in my head about the built-in hazards of being a pastor's spouse. I replayed the difficulties of hurts, staff crises, unreasonable expectations, personal growth challenges, and relationship disappointments. They became my reference point for the

...sent and future. When I learned that the future did ...ot have to be more of the past, I began to do some things differently.

I carved out time in my life for overnight retreats with God and recreation. I pursued things that I loved, such as the outdoors. Our family moved. Pete and I went for help for our marriage. We learned skills to help us in our relationship. I set boundaries with Pete and his work. I set limits around what I would and would not do at New Life. I became realistic about how many relationships I could handle. And I said no frequently.

When you find yourself caught in the quicksand of faulty thinking, ask yourself two questions:

1. Am I willing to stop doing the familiar thing that isn't working and try something that feels unfamiliar but may be more likely to succeed?
2. What will I regret twenty years from now if I don't get up and do something to change my situation?

Each of my "Quits" initially required that I do something radically different, and all of them felt uncomfortable in the beginning. Don't underestimate how difficult it is to take this counterintuitive, countercultural step.

"If at first you don't succeed, do something different!"

Often, everything in us is screaming, "Don't risk change. This could result in a disaster!"

When an unhealthy pattern is deeply ingrained in our lives, it's difficult to do something different by our own efforts alone. When I have struggled with clarity on what to do differently, I sought outside help from mentors, counselors, or spiritual directors. This has served me well over the years. We often need help from someone more experienced to help us see our situation more objectively.

You may know the old adage, "If at first you don't succeed, try, try again." That motto needs an adaptation to "If at first you don't succeed, do something different!" But you will need right thinking, realistic thinking, and a plan to make changes for your future.

Sailing with the Wind

A couple of years ago, Pete and I had our first experience learning to sail. One of the most important things we learned was to position the sail in the right spot in order to go forward. For beginners, this is harder than it looks. When the sail is not congruent with the wind, there are three possibilities: you go around in circles, you are stuck and don't move at all, or you tip over. Faulty thinking is like having the sail in the wrong position. You can't go forward. You are stuck simply recycling the same pains, frustrations, and problems.

Busting through the wall of faulty thinking launches you forward in life-transforming ways. The radical mental adjustment of quitting faulty thinking enlarges your sail. It positions your sail correctly so it can be moved freely by the wind. Ultimately, that wind is the Holy Spirit, who corrects your faulty thinking and aligns it with the truth.

As we will see, courage to walk out your unique life requires examining closely the life you are now living.

you living your life or someone else's? If you don't ke responsibility for living your God-given life, it will not get lived. There is no one else in the world like you. No one! One of the greatest ways you honor and glorify God is through embracing your unrepeatable life. For this reason, to quit living someone else's life is the topic of the final chapter.

8

Quit Living
Someone Else's Life

Six months after Pete and I married, we moved to Central America for one year to learn Spanish. Toward the end of that year, Pete arranged for us to visit Nicaragua at the end of their civil war between the Sandinistas and the Contras.

"Won't this be incredible?" he argued persuasively, "Now we speak the language and know a family in the capital, Managua, who can show us around!"

I was six months pregnant with our first daughter, so this wasn't high on my list of vacation spots, but I went along nonetheless.

Because of the war, a single bus entered the country only once a week. So on a humid Tuesday morning we boarded an old greyhound bus from Costa Rica for the all-day trip through the mountains. Only seven others were on that bus, all mothers who had brought their sons to Costa Rica to avoid fighting in the war. Each carried oversized suitcases brimming over with toilet paper and other goods impossible to buy in Nicaragua.

After a three-hour delay, our bus finally left.

The driver drove fast, very fast. When we entered the mountainous region approaching Nicaragua, he picked up speed as if he were driving a Ferrari. The only problem was that none of the mountainous roads had guardrails. My initial discomfort with his speed quickly turned from fright to outright panic.

His speed was not my speed.

I stumbled toward the front to the bus, begging him in my limited Spanish to slow down. He ignored me.

I pleaded with him again—to no avail.

I don't do well with heights, even when driving slowly or hiking on bridges. This was in another category altogether.

I got down on my knees and prayed.

I sat on the floor with my head between my legs.

I cried. He raced on.

Pete yelled at him to slow down. Nothing.

Finally I prayed, "Okay, God, I know this is the end. Please make it quick."

The bus felt out of control. The driver was oblivious both to me and the other passengers. I waited for the moment when we would lunge over a cliff.

Then it happened.

The bus broke down.

The bus driver quickly opened the hood to examine the smoking engine, shaking his head saying, "Muy grave" (very serious). He paced back and forth alongside the bus. About an hour later, a truck stopped, and he got a ride, informing us he was not coming back.

I remember like it was yesterday, sitting on the grass

in the middle of nowhere. We were many miles from our destination, abandoned by that bus driver. And I was experiencing one of the happiest moments of my life!

I had my life back. I was thrilled.

We walked, hitchhiked, and taxied our way to the capital of Nicaragua, but that adventure is a story for another time. My point here is how that experience illustrates the first eight years of my married life—a season in which I felt like I was living everyone's life except my own.

Our first eight years of married life—learning Spanish in Central America, moving to New York City, having children, starting a church in Queens—were a roller-coaster ride in which I was hanging on for dear life. I was in the back of an out-of-control bus driven by someone else, and I felt powerless to get off. Sadly, it took a "near death" experience for me to tell Pete I wanted to get off that bus.

Whose Life Are You Living?

Toward the end of his life, Irish playwright George Bernard Shaw was asked what person in history he would most like to have been. He responded by saying he would most like to have been the George Bernard Shaw he might have become but never did.

How about you? Whose life are you living—your own or someone else's? The following are a few signs to help you discern if you are living someone else's life:

- You care too much what others think of you.
- You lie.
- You blame.

- You avoid confrontation.
- You believe false peace is better than no peace.
- You always put others before yourself.
- You say yes, even when you don't want to.
- You can't disagree with strong people.
- You are more concerned with keeping people happy at the expense of your own happiness.
- You are unsure of your preferences.

Are you driving the bus of your life or, without really realizing it, have you surrendered the steering wheel to someone else?

God calls us to get off the bus other people are driving. Jesus did.

When he asserted himself in his hometown of Nazareth, declaring himself as the Messiah, his neighbors and lifelong friends literally tried to throw him off a cliff. He passed through them to walk out faithfully the life the Father had crafted for him (Luke 4:28–31).

When the crowds shouted, "Hosanna, save us," and wanted to appoint Jesus as their king, he ignored their praises, knowing their agenda for his life was not his Father's will (John 6:14–15).

God calls us to get off the bus other people are driving.

On more than one occasion, Jesus disappointed his mother and siblings (Mark 3:21), his disciples, the crowds, and the religious leaders (John 6:41–62).

The pressure on Jesus to live someone else's life was enormous. Yet, by the power of the Holy Spirit and in communion with God, he stayed true to his own life and purpose, finishing the work the Father had given him (John 17:4).

In the same way, God invites you and me to ignore the distracting voices around us—regardless of their source—and to pursue wholeheartedly our God-given life. When we do, we and ultimately everyone around us experience a newfound freedom.

Discovering Yourself—A Life Work

Church reformer and theologian John Calvin argued that there is no more exalted a description of a Christian than this: "We are God's handiwork" (lit., "masterpiece"; Ephesians 2:10). Galaxies, stars, and solar systems can knock us breathless with God's glory (Psalm 19:1), but only human beings who have experienced the miracle of a new birth are called God's masterpiece.

Masterpieces aren't made by run-of-the-mill craftsmen; they require the skilled hands of a genius. They are one-of-a-kind, never-to-be-repeated gifts to the world. And that's what you are, God's one-of-a-kind, never-to-be-repeated gift to the world. God the Creator made you unique. Your beauty as a divine masterpiece, however, has been damaged by sin. The restoration process is lifelong, slow, and costly.

Michelangelo's Sistine Chapel is one of history's greatest artistic triumphs. From 1508 to 1512, the artist lay on his back and painted the creation, fall, and destruction of the human race by the flood. The images, however, started to fade almost immediately after he painted them. Within a hundred years no one remembered what the original colors really had looked like. In 1980, a scaffold was erected and plans made to clean the ceiling of

Michelangelo's priceless masterpiece. The director of the restoration project did a critical experiment using a special solution on one or two square inches at a time.

For the next twelve years they cleaned the entire ceiling of the Sistine Chapel. No one expected the results to be so stunning! No one realized Michelangelo was such a master of color—of azure, green, rose, lavender. Beneath centuries of grime and dirt, passionate colors lay buried. For the first time in over 450 years, people could view the masterpiece as it was originally intended, in all its color and beauty.[1]

Stripping off the false layers and dirt that cover up your unique destiny and life is complex. Parker Palmer describes it like this:

> Most of us arrive at a sense of self only through a long journey through alien lands. But this journey bears no resemblance to the trouble-free "travel packages" sold by the tourism industry. It is more akin to the ancient tradition of pilgrimage—"a transformative journey to a sacred center" full of hardship, darkness and peril.[2]

Another way to discern our distinctive life is from the perspective of discovering our "sealed orders" from God.[3] Sealed orders, historically, referred to specific written instructions given, for example, to the captain of a ship regarding his destination or mission. They are not to be opened until a specified time or place is reached. It is as if God has given each one of us sealed orders for our lives. He invites us to open them by paying attention to the little everyday things that give us life. Author Sheila Linn simply and profoundly describes this process: "When I am in touch with the special purpose of my life in carrying out my sealed orders, I have a profound feeling of consolation or rightness and my whole body relaxes. I believe the sense of rightness expresses itself physiologically because the purpose of our life is built into the very cells of our body."[4]

> *It is as if God has given each one of us sealed orders for our lives.*

Discovering God's special purpose for your life is a process. It's impossible to anticipate everything we might encounter on this journey to an authentic self and a healthy spirituality. I've discovered four practices that provide trustworthy guidance for this journey: discover your integrity, listen to your inner rhythm, set boundaries, and let go of others. As you apply these practices, you will join an adventure with God around the joy of fulfilling your special purpose on earth.

Discover Your Integrity

The journey of living your life instead of someone else's begins when you discover your integrity. This requires recognizing and defining what is important to you. Integrity, as I use it here, is always aligned with God's values. For example, although your integrity may require you to leave an abusive relationship, it does not require that you abandon your spouse simply because you no longer feel sure you love him.

When helping someone who is struggling with an inner conflict, I often ask, "What is your integrity calling you to do?" Most people hesitate before responding because they have rarely thought deeply about what they believe and value. They have seldom considered the dissonance between their outer and inner life, between their actions and their values.

The question behind that question is this: "What is important to you?" If you do not take the time to answer that question, other people's fears, expectations, and agendas (or even your own fears) will drive you. You will end up defining yourself by what you are against rather than what is most significant to you.

Throughout my years at New Life, honoring my integrity has repeatedly called me to evaluate my commitments. For example, I was once actively pursued to attend a milestone birthday celebration for a woman in our church. She emailed me, wrote me a letter, called, and spoke to me on a Sunday to reinforce her desire for me to attend. But I was clear about the importance of time with my family and daughters that year. During that season in my life, my integrity called me to pull back from social activities to be more present and involved with my children. This availability enabled me to have many significant conversations and teachable moments with them; I enjoyed unhurried time with them as they worked through their inner conflicts and struggles. This would not have happened had I failed to honor my integrity and bowed to pressure from others to fill up my calendar with their events.

If I say yes to this person or commitment, will I be a more, or less, loving person?

There are many other things integrity has called me to do. Honoring my integrity has called me to ...

- confront Pete on inconsistencies in himself and his leadership at New Life.

- pursue additional training in emotional health, marriage issues, and theology to meet the ministry demands of helping increasing numbers of people inside and outside New Life.

- create a life that reflects the values Pete and I teach around emotionally healthy spirituality. In other words, we don't want to teach what we are not living.

- invest time and money consistently into our marriage. This includes getaway weekends as well as formal and informal training with mentors, relationship educators, and therapists.

- craft a home that eliminates unnecessary waste by living simply. We use water bottles instead of bottled water, cloth rather than paper napkins. We removed our television over twelve years ago and now watch only DVDs we choose to bring into our home.

Stand firm, not caving in when misunderstood. When all is said and done, nothing is more important than being faithful to the will of the Father and growing in love. When I overextend myself or start doing things God has not asked me to do, my capacity to love shrinks. I often ask myself, "If I say yes to this person or commitment, will I be a more, or less, loving person?"

Ultimately, it takes less energy to live from a place where we are actively identifying what's important to us than to live in continuous reaction to the expectations and demands of others.

Listen to Your Inner Rhythm

All creation has a natural rhythm. This is part of God's handiwork in the universe. We have night and day, winter and summer, and the great movements of seas and stars. All living things have an internal rhythm, an internal clock hardwired into them, so that they might thrive in healthy, balanced ways. Our bodies, for example, have rhythms for sleeping, eating, and breathing. When we ignore this wonderful gift from God and work seventy hours a week, skim on our sleep, skip meals, or push our bodies beyond their limits, we suffer.

The same principle applies to the emotional and spiritual rhythms of our lives. If I neglect my relationship with God, if I go beyond my people limits, if I don't nurture delight and joy, my soul begins to die. I get depressed. When we do finally stop and rest, our natural rhythms reassert themselves and return us back to God's intended balance. But in the rush and pressure of our lives, it is easy to not listen or respect our rhythms.

In the rush and pressure of our lives, it is easy to not listen or respect our rhythms.

At the same time, we each have different rhythms. Our internal clocks have variations. What is optimal for you will not be optimal for those around you.

Rhythm has to do with timing—when it is time to engage or disengage, to remain or to transition, to be with people or be apart, to work or to rest, to play or to be serious. Jesus paid attention and honored his rhythms. He knew when it was time to move on to another town. He knew when he needed to be alone. He knew when he needed to be with three people or five thousand. He knew when it was time to preach and when it was time to pray.

In the morning, I sense the rightness of exercising first and then being still before God. In the evening, my inner clock tells me, "It is best to first talk with Pete and then read before going to sleep." Pete's rhythm is the opposite of mine. He prefers being still before God first in the morning and then exercise. In the evening, his inner clock tells him, "It is best to read first and then talk with Geri before going to sleep." We had to learn, over time, to respect and negotiate our different rhythms.

My mother is an amazing person with an enormous capacity for extending hospitality to large numbers of people. It is not uncommon for her to have a spontaneous dinner for twenty people in her home in the summer. And she is eighty-five years old! Her inner rhythm frequently says it is time for a house full of people. In our early years of marriage, I tried to live her rhythms. Between out-of-town guests, small groups, socials, and our daughters' friends, a steady stream of guests poured into our home. Yet I struggled, not appreciating that my rhythms were different. Only years later did I acknowledge my need for solitude was much greater than my mother's.

Honoring our different rhythms involves respecting and negotiating our needs and preferences at work, with friends, at church, in our marriage, our extended families, and even our parenting.

To begin listening to your inner rhythms, consider the following questions: Do you know when it is time to be with people and when it is time to be alone? Do you know when it is time to rest or time to play? What are your most optimal work hours? How much sleep do you need? When is it time to eat? Is it time for you to wait on something or is it time to move on? How does the pace of your life feel? What can you do to establish an enjoyable routine and healthy balance in this season of your life? And finally, what are one or two changes you can make in order to get more in step with your God-given inner rhythms?

Set Your Boundaries

With whom do you need to set boundaries? The answer is simple: with everyone! This includes your mother, father, siblings, spouse, children, friends, coworkers, even your pet! Boundaries are crucial if you are to avoid detours and follow God's path for you.[5]

It's not bad that people want what they want. People will always want things from you — your time, your emotional support, your expertise, your money, your participation, whatever it is that you have that they want. This is normal.

With whom do you need to set boundaries? The answer is simple: with everyone!

It also does not make them bad. We all want what we want — even nice, giving people like you! However, the fact that someone wants something from you does not necessarily mean God wants *you* to provide it or that he wants them to have it. Of course, it is often easier to do what others want and be who they want, but the question is: What is best in the long run?

What is best in the long run is for you and me to set boundaries in order to be faithful to our God-given lives.

Otherwise, we end up fused to others. *Fusion* is a term from physics that describes what happens when metals are melted together and lose their distinctive qualities. Emotional fusion happens when we lose our distinctiveness and lose ourselves in someone else's life.[6]

Pete is a multigifted leader with countless creative ideas. He has a large capacity for juggling many responsibilities at the same time. When I fail to set my boundaries around his work, however, I begin to feel like I'm on a roller-coaster ride hanging on for my life. Being married to him naturally tends to pull me into his numerous projects. If I am not careful, before I know it, I lose myself in trying to juggle his different initiatives. I have learned to recognize my limits and, therefore, choose my yes's and no's prayerfully and thoughtfully.

Think over your commitments—in your church community and in your marriage, with friends, children, neighbors, coworkers, and extended family members. What problems or commitments might you have taken on that God never intended? In what relationship(s) do you need to establish a healthier boundary today? What might that look like? What support will you need in prayer and from others? How can you keep this boundary from becoming a wall that keeps you from loving others?

Remember, we set boundaries to love people well. And in setting ourselves free to live our life, we are setting those around us free as well.

Let Go of Others

To quit living someone else's life requires not only healthy boundaries with others, but also not trying to run other people's lives. In letting go, I do not run interference in the lives of others. Controlling the lives of others takes time and energy; it also takes the focus off your own life.

When others think, feel, and act differently than we do, we tend to become anxious. This creates a gravitational pull to want to control them. If you're a parent, you know how challenging this can be.

I nursed, fed, clothed, and kept our four daughters alive throughout their childhoods. They literally depended on me for their lives, and I naturally thought of them as an extension of myself. Yet, one of my God-given tasks is to intentionally nurture their separateness from me.

I remember when, in high school, one of my daughters wanted to spend eighty-five dollars on a pair of shoes. I said, "That's crazy. Please don't spend that much money on one pair of shoes." I felt stressed and anxious. Where was this going to lead? She was violating so many of my values—about good management and budgeting of money, the question of how many pairs of shoes are morally appropriate for one person to own, and the moral "correctness" of spending so much money on one pair of shoes.

Despite my protests, she assured me they were a good investment.

My daughter did buy those shoes and eventually handed them down to me. Now, six years later, they remain among my favorite and most frequently worn shoes. I remember thinking, "Hmmm, maybe I can learn some things about quality shopping from my daughter." This was an important lesson for me: her preferences are not only different from but sometimes wiser than mine.

Letting go and respecting differences with our children is an ongoing process. Just because I am cold does not mean they are cold. Just because I am thirsty on a hot day does not mean they are thirsty. I may love the outdoors and exercising, but that does not mean they do. I preferred to paint their room pink and wanted our daughters to learn a musical instrument. They wanted different color schemes for their bedrooms and showed little interest in music lessons.

As children become teenagers and young adults, letting go requires releasing increasing amounts of control over whom they date and marry, their choice of careers, what colleges they attend, and their decisions about following Christ. Please do not misunderstand—I believe parents play a vital role in coaching children toward good choices. If a child is involved in behavior that is hurting them or others, it is a parent's responsibility to intervene. But there are many areas of life where our kids make choices that aren't wrong; they are simply different from the ones we might make.

Finally, when they are adults, and perhaps married, we are challenged to watch them raise their children differently than we raised them. We do our best to make a mature transition from being their parents to being their peers, giving advice and counsel only when asked.

Letting others go, however, crosses over into more areas of life than just parenting. For example, we think people should know how to dress or act in church and how to nurture their spiritual lives. People make choices to leave our spiritual community and join another. We can become resentful or we can appreciate that their journey is different from ours. People see political and international issues differently than I do. I can listen and ask questions, seeking to understand, or I can become angry at what I perceive as narrowness.

One of the litmus tests to discern my spiritual growth in letting go is to detect when traces of resentment and judgmentalism prevail in my heart rather than an appreciation of differences. I can pronounce: "Well, if Pete wants to spend a beautiful Saturday in a library reading a book, that's his choice. I won't say a word, even though he is missing out on God's gift of being outside!" Or I can pause and genuinely appreciate how unique he is: "I am sad that I am going on a hike alone this afternoon, but Pete's ability to learn and read in so many diverse areas is a wonder to behold."

When, where, and with whom do you need to let go? When are you tempted to think you know best when it is really only a matter of preference? Name one or two areas where you can let go of a decision someone made that you are anxious about. Prayerfully commit this person and situation to the Lord. How might God be using this process of letting go to prepare you for something new he has for you?

Write Your Manifesto

A few years back I wrote my manifesto—a public declaration of my beliefs and values—as the culmination of a series of retreats I had been involved in over a two-year period. Drawing from a compilation of poems, essays, and Scriptures, I attempted to summarize and clarify my thirty-year journey with Christ. Like putting together the pieces of a puzzle, I began to see the larger picture of my life—past, present, and future. I sensed that the unique colors of my own personal journey longed to shine forth through layers of old paint covering over my true self in Christ.

I slowly put these down on paper and later pinned it on the wall in front of my desk, where it remains to this day. I am a work in progress. Yet it turned out to be another important step to quit living someone else's life and to take up my own.

This is my personal manifesto, expressing my beliefs and values. You may want to craft your own. But I share these with you to give you an idea of the direction you may want to go in. These truths were custom fit to a particular stage in my journey. But they may spark ways in which God wants to uniquely speak to you in yours.

- Love the Lord your God with all your heart, mind, soul, and strength by loving what you love.[7]
- Love your neighbor not better than yourself, not above yourself, but *as* yourself.
- Walk humbly, love mercy, and do justice (see Micah 6:8)—and you don't have to walk on your knees for a hundred miles through the desert to do so![8]
- Taste and see that the Lord is good by enjoying the joy of marriage, the love and laughter of family, good food and drink, the warmth of the sun, the feel of your body gliding through the water, the fragrance and colors of herbs and flowers, a star-filled night, and the image of God in every person.
- Respect your God-given limits and grow through your false-self limits, or you can do others great damage.[9]

- Treat silence as a best friend.
- When the going gets rough, turn to wonder.
- Be quick to ask questions and be slow to advise.
- My first work is to set my heart at rest, to be still and know that he is God.
- There are "treasures in darkness. It holdeth riches past computing."[10]
- She who is not happy cannot help many people.
- Remember the wisdom of the deer. Just be, imperfections and all.[11]
- Treat every thought and feeling—no matter how joyful or dark—as a guest because each one has been sent to guide me.[12]
- Remember the loaves and the fishes: God is the Source of my life (John 6:1–13).
- Remember the salmon: Don't turn away from the hit, turn toward it to experience mystery and grace.

This final line in my manifesto reminds me that deciding to quit living someone else's life often feels like that of a salmon swimming against a powerful current. When salmons prepare to mate, they swim upstream, up waterfalls seeming to defy gravity. Salmon somehow know how to turn their undersides—from center to tail—into the powerful current coming at them. It hits them squarely, and the impact then launches them out and farther up the waterfall. They do this over and over again until they actually climb over the waterfall. The particular way they lean into the current actually bounces them farther and farther up in the air. From a distance, it seems as if these fish are actually flying.

When you discover your integrity, listen to your inner rhythms, set boundaries, and let go, like the salmon, you push against strong currents in yourself and in our culture. The miracle is that when you do these things, you climb up and over a powerful waterfall that threatens to sweep you away. And you enter into the joy of your own beautifully God-given life, where you now carry out your own God-given "sealed orders."

Choose to Live Divided No More[13]

You may have come to this book looking for solutions to some problems. Perhaps you were captured by the title *The Emotionally Healthy Woman*, secretly hoping it would give you three easy steps to become whole. My interest, however, has been in providing you with a fresh vision for transformation in Christ and a few powerful principles for rethinking misunderstood biblical truths.

I am, thankfully, a very different person from what I was when I first quit our church many years ago. It has been enormously liberating to stop pretending and to choose to do something different, to choose life over death.

My greatest goal is authentic love—love of God, myself, and others. Practicing these eight "Quits" has been one of the most significant means to that end. And I will continue to practice them, allowing God to use them to transform me the rest of my life.

The "Quits" brought me out of illusion into reality, out of darkness into light, out of deception into truth, out of inner bondage into interior freedom, out of sadness into joy, out of fear into peace, out of hate into love, out of blindness into sight. I don't know many things, but as the blind man who received his sight from Jesus said, "One thing I do know. I was blind but now I see" (John 9:25).

My invitation, in closing, is to invite you to make a Rosa Parks decision regarding your life today, to become the unique woman God has crafted you to be. As an African-American woman living in the segregated South in the 1950s, Rosa Parks was tired of pretending everything was fine when it was not. Quaker author Parker J. Palmer recounts her story as follows:

> On December 1, 1955, in Montgomery, Alabama, Rosa Parks did something she was not supposed to do: she sat down at the front of a bus in one of the seats reserved for whites — a dangerous, daring, and provocative act in a racist society. [When asked,] "Why did you sit down at the front of the bus that day?" Rosa Parks did not say that she sat down to launch a movement ... She said, "I sat down because I was tired." She meant that her soul was tired, her heart was tired, her whole being was tired.[14]

Rosa Parks made a decision that day to live divided no more. She would no longer live on the outside what contradicted the truth of her integrity on the inside. She refused to smile on the outside while being sad on the inside.

This is what I pray that you also will choose to do. May you take hold of God's courage to live divided no more, discovering the Spirit's supernatural power that yearns to break into your life and birth that which is new and beautiful.

And remember: It is never too late to start quitting.

Notes

Introduction: When You Can't Take It Anymore

1. Joe Simpson, *Touching the Void: The True Story of One Man's Miraculous Survival* (New York: HarperCollins, 2004), 120–21, 126. My account is also based on interviews with the two climbers in the film *Touching the Void*.

Chapter 1: Quit Being Afraid of What Others Think

1. G. R. Evans, trans., *Bernard of Clairvaux: Selected Works*, Classics of Western Spirituality (Mahwah, NJ: Paulist Press, 1987), 173–205.
2. This is adapted from David Schnarch, *Resurrecting Sex* (New York: HarperCollins, 2003), 120–21.
3. Paul was reminding Peter of the essence of the gospel. God accepts sinners through faith in Jesus Christ alone and through his finished work on the cross. This is the way of salvation for all sinners, Jews and Gentiles alike.
4. Parker J. Palmer, *Let Your Life Speak: Listening to the Voice of Vocation* (San Francisco: Jossey Bass, 2000), 56–72.
5. A specific skill we have developed to walk out this truth is called: "Climb the Ladder of Integrity." See Session 6 in Pete and Geri Scazzero, *Emotionally Healthy Skills 2.0: Transform the Way You Love God, Yourselves, and Others* (Elmhurst, NY: Emotionally Healthy Spirituality, 2012). This is available at www.emotionally healthy.org or the Emotionally Healthy Spirituality App through the Apple iTunes store.

Chapter 2: Quit Lying

1. Virginia Satir, John Banmen, Jane Gerber, and Maria Gomori, *The Satir Model: Family Therapy and Beyond* (Palo Alto, CA: Science and Behavior Books, 1991), 301.
2. www.livescience.com/health/060515_why_lie.html
3. Sue Monk Kidd, *When the Heart Waits: Spiritual Direction for Life's Sacred Questions* (New York: Harper Collins, 1990), 163.
4. Sandra Wilson, *Released from Shame: Moving Beyond the Pain of the Past* (Downers Grove, IL: InterVarsity Press, 1990), 78.

Chapter 3: Quit Dying to the Wrong Things

1. In 2 Timothy 1:8 Paul writes, "Join with me in suffering for the gospel, by the power of God."
2. For a well-rounded biblical explanation on the gift of limits, see chapter 8, "Receive the Gift of Limits," by Pete Scazzero, *The Emotionally Healthy Church: Updated and Expanded Edition* (Grand Rapids: Zondervan, 2010).
3. Henri J. M. Nouwen, *The Return of the Prodigal Son: A Meditation on Fathers, Brothers and Sons* (New York: Doubleday, 1992), 101.
4. We highly recommend the following book as helpful to the *Prayer of Examen*: Dennis Linn, Sheila Fabricant Linn, and Matthew Linn, *Sleeping with Bread: Holding What Gives You Life* (Mahwah, NJ: Paulist Press, 1995).
5. Eugene H. Peterson, *Eat This Book: A Conversation in the Art of Spiritual Reading* (Grand Rapids: Eerdmans, 2006), 71.
6. David had to die to his lies, his adultery, when Nathan the prophet confronts him in 2 Samuel 11–12. He also had to die to his pride when he placed his trust in his military power rather than God in the powerful account of his counting of his fighting men in 1 Chronicles 21:1–17.
7. For a more detailed understanding of this, go to Peter Scazzero, *The Emotionally Healthy Church*.
8. I encourage you to consider using any number of helpful tools that are available—the 16PF (Personality Factors), the MMPI, DISC, Myers-Briggs.
9. You may also want to consider the questionnaire developed by Don Richard Riso and Russ Hudson, *The Riso-Hudson Enneagram Type Indicator* (Stone Ridge, NY: Enneagram Institute, 2000), or www.enneagraminstitute.com for an online version

10. See Richard Rohr, *The Enneagram: A Christian Perspective* (New York: Crossroad, 2001); Renee Baron and Elizabeth Wagele, *The Enneagram Made Easy: Discover the 9 Types of People* (San Francisco: HarperSanFrancisco, 1994).

Chapter 4: Quit Denying Anger, Sadness, and Fear

1. Aristotle. Cited at www.wisdomquotes.com/quote/aristotle-10.html.
2. Adapted from Michael Yapko's lectures found in *Calm Down! A Self-Help Program for Managing Anxiety* (Audio CD program) (Fallbrook, CA: Yapko Publications, 2008).
3. Henri J. M. Nouwen, *Can You Drink the Cup?* (Notre Dame, IN: Ave Maria, 1996).
4. For a fuller explanation and model of how to begin to pay attention to you anger, sadness, and fear, see Session 4, "Explore the Iceberg," in *Emotionally Healthy Spirituality 2.0*, by Pete and Geri Scazzero. Also downloadable from the Emotionally Healthy Spirituality App, available through the Apple iTunes store.

Chapter 5: Quit Blaming

1. Virginia Satir developed what she called the Self-Esteem Maintenance Tool Kit. See Satir, Banmen, Gerber, and Gomori, *The Satir Model*, 293–97.
2. Peter L. Steinke, *Congregational Leadership in Anxious Times: Being Calm and Courageous No Matter What* (Herndon, VA: Alban Institute, 2006), 81.
3. For a fuller explanation of Sabbath, see Pete's explanation of Sabbath in Pete Scazzero, *Emotionally Healthy Spirituality: Unleash a Revolution in Your Life in Christ* (Nashville, TN: Nelson, 2006), 165–73.

Chapter 6: Quit Overfunctioning

1. The poem "Millie's Mother's Red Dress," by Carol Lynn Pearson (www.clpearson.com), is published in the anthology *Beginnings and Beyond*, published by Cedar Fort Press (Cedar Fort, Utah, 2005). Used by permission.
2. For an excellent discussion on overfunctioning, see Harriet Goldhor Lerner, *The Dance of Intimacy: A Woman's Guide to Courageous*

Acts to Change in Key Relationships (New York: Harper and Row, 1989), 102–22.

3. This was cited from a lecture given by Ed Friedman, available at www.leadershipinministry.com/may_i_help_you%3F.htm

Chapter 7: Quit Faulty Thinking

1. Pastoring, supervising, and mentoring involve spiritual authority and are teacher/advisor relationships. Being one's employer also carries with it a level of authority and power. Friendship is quite different. Expectations and demands are minimal. Power and authority are distributed equally and evenly. The boundaries are different. Friendship belongs more with peers and not so much in a relationship of teaching or advising.

2. We model and describe the skill "Stop Mind Reading" in Lesson 2 of *Emotionally Healthy Skills 2.0*, by Pete and Geri Scazzero. Also downloadable from the Emotionally Healthy Spirituality App, available through the Apple iTunes store.

3. A great deal of research has been done on higher modes (the high road) of brain processing that involve rational, reflective thought over against lower mode (or low road) processing that is more impulsive, reactive, and lacking in self-reflection. For more information, see Daniel J. Seigel and Mary Hartzell, *Parenting from the Inside Out: How a Deeper Self-Understanding Can Help You Raise Children Who Thrive* (New York: Penguin, 2003), 154–219, and Daniel Seigel, *The Mindful Brain: Reflection and Attunement in the Cultivation of Well-Being* (New York: Norton, 2007).

Chapter 8: Quit Living Someone Else's Life

1. Al Janseen, Gary Rosberg, and Barbara Rosberg, *Your Marriage Masterpiece: Discovering God's Amazing Design for Your Life Together* (Wheaton, IL: Tyndale, 2008), 15–18.

2. Palmer, *Let Your Life Speak*, 17–18.

3. This is a term used by Agnes Sanford, *Sealed Orders* (Alachua, FL: Bridge-Logos, 1972).

4. Dennis Linn, Sheila Fabricant Linn, and Matthew Linn, *Sleeping with Bread: Holding What Gives You Life* (Mahwah, NJ: Paulist Press, 1995), 21.

5. See Michael D. Yapko, *Breaking the Patterns of Depression* (New York: Broad Books, Random House, 1997), 284–320.
6. Steinke, *Congregational Leadership in Anxious Times*, 26.
7. This idea came to me as a result of the influence of Mary Oliver's poem "Wild Geese." It can be found at: www.english.illinois.edu/MAPS/poets/m_r/oliver/online_poems.htm. Loving what you love is a way to bring glory to God.
8. This is also from Mary Oliver's poem "Wild Geese." Suffering for suffering's sake does not make us good. Jesus desires mercy, not sacrifice (Matthew 9:13).
9. For a discussion on discerning the difference between God-given limits we are to receive and limits that God is asking me to break through, see Scazzero, *The Emotionally Healthy Church*, chapter 8 (pp. 137–58).
10. This is a line from a Helen Keller poem entitled "Once in Regions Void of Light." It can be found at: www.abadeo.com/books/keller.html. The phrase "treasures in darkness" comes from Isaiah 45:3, which reads, "I will give you the treasures of darkness, riches stored in secret places."
11. This line comes from a poem entitled "The Wisdom of the Deer," by Kent Osborne. The wisdom of the deer is to be present to one's own dignity and the beauty of one's whole story. Present knowledge of oneself is a treasure, imperfections and all.
12. This comes from a poem by Rumi entitled "The Guest House." www.panhala.net/Archive/The_Guest_House.html.
13. I first learned this helpful term from Parker Palmer, *A Hidden Wholeness: The Journey toward an Undivided Life* (San Francisco: Jossey Bass, 2004).
14. Palmer, *Let Your Life Speak*, 32–33.

The Emotionally Healthy Woman Small Group Curriculum
by Geri and Peter Scazzero

Developing an emotionally healthy spiritual life, one that explores and transforms the parts of us that often remain hidden deep beneath the surface, begins with quitting. Chains break inside of us when we finally say, "No more. I quit!" We are then freed up to choose new ways of being with, and living for, God. This is the far-reaching premise of the groundbreaking book *The Emotionally Healthy Woman* and its companion workbook and DVD.

Each component of *The Emotionally Healthy Woman Small Group Curriculum* works together to guide you through the deep integration of profound biblical truths with your personal life, relationships, and church.

The topics covered include:

Quit Being Afraid of What Others Think

Quit Lying

Quit Dying to the Wrong Things

Quit Denying Anger, Sadness, and Fear

Quit Blaming

Quit Over-Functioning

Quit Faulty Thinking

Quit Living Someone Else's Life

AVAILABLE AT **EMOTIONALLYHEALTHY.ORG**.

Transform the way you love God, yourself, and others!

Emotionally Healthy Skills 2.0

This groundbreaking curriculum, the fruit of sixteen years of research and development, is designed to provide the necessary practical tools for your spiritual journey so that you can grow into a spiritually and emotionally mature follower of Jesus.

Each session is designed to teach you new Scripture-based skills, and how to integrate them into your friendships, small group, family, workplace, neighborhood, and church.

Emotionally Healthy Skills Sessions:
1: Introduction and Community Temperature Reading
2: Stop Mind Reading and Clarify Expectations
3: Genogram Your Family
4: Explore the Iceberg
5: Incarnational Listening
6: Climb the Ladder of Integrity
7: Clean Fighting
8: Develop a Rule of Life to Implement Emotionally Healthy Skills

AVAILABLE AT **EMOTIONALLYHEALTHY.ORG**.

Emotionally Healthy Spirituality App

for iPhone & iPad

Looking for a way to support your transformational journey?

The Emotionally Healthy Spirituality app is your personal guide to emotional and spiritual growth. Downloading this app gives you instant access to teaching and tools from best-selling author Peter Scazzero.

IN-APP PURCHASES UNLOCK:
- **The automated EHS Inventory Test to measure your emotional health**

- *Emotionally Healthy Skills 2.0* **video sessions**

FREE CONTENT INCLUDES:
• Preview of Peter Scazzero's best-selling, ground-breaking work book *Emotionally Healthy Spirituality*

weeks of newly published Daily Office to encourage you about the day

bscriptions

content on emotionally healthy leadership and

from Peter Scazzero to

s QR code to access the app on your smartphone.

The Emotionally Healthy Church

A Strategy for Discipleship That Actually Changes Lives

Peter L. Scazzero with Warren Bird

In this revised and expanded edition of his Gold Medallion Award-winning book, Scazzero shares refreshing new insights and a different and challenging slant on what it takes to lead your congregation to wholeness and maturity in Christ.

Sharing from New Life Fellowship's painful but liberating journey, Scazzero reveals exactly how the truth can and does make you free — not just superficially, but deep down. This expanded edition of *The Emotionally Healthy Church* not only takes the original six principles further and deeper, but also adds a seventh crucial principle. You'll acquire knowledge and tools that can help you and others:

- look beneath the surface of problems
- break the power of past wounds, failures, sins, and circumstances
- live a life of brokenness and vulnerability
- recognize and honor personal limitations and boundaries
- embrace grief and loss
- make incarnation your model to love others
- slow down to lead with integrity

... edition shares powerful insights on how contemplative spiri-... help you and your church slow down—an integral key to ... motional health. Open these pages and find out how ... rn a new corner on the road to spiritual maturity.

... able in stores and online!

ZONDERVAN®
.com

The Emotionally Healthy Church Workbook

8 Studies for Groups or Individuals

Peter L. Scazzero

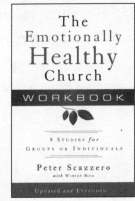

Emotional health and spiritual maturity are inseparable: that is the premise of the award-winning book *The Emotionally Healthy Church*. This stand-alone workbook helps leaders and lay persons alike apply the biblical truths in Peter Scazzero's revolutionary book to their personal lives, small groups, and churches. Eight studies take you beyond merely reading about emotional health to actually cultivating it as a disciple of Jesus. Step by step, you'll discover what it means to have Christ transform the deep places hidden beneath the surface so that you might become more authentic and loving toward God, others, and yourself.

Available in stores and online!

WILLOW
Willow Creek Association
Vision, Training, Resources for Prevailing Churches

This resource was created to serve you and to help you build a local church that prevails. It is just one of many ministry tools published by the Willow Creek Association.

The Willow Creek Association (WCA) was created in 1992 to serve a rapidly growing number of churches from across the denominational spectrum that are committed to helping unchurched people become fully devoted followers of Christ. Membership in the WCA now numbers over 12,000 Member Churches worldwide from more than ninety denominations.

The Willow Creek Association links like-minded Christian leaders with each other and with strategic vision, training and resources in order to help them build prevailing churches designed to reach their redemptive potential.

For specific information about WCA conferences, resources, membership and other ministry services contact:

Willow Creek Association
P.O. Box 3188
Barrington, IL 60011-3188
Phone: 847.570.9812
Fax: 847.765.5046
www.willowcreek.com

Share Your Thoughts

With the Author: Your comments will be forwarded to the author when you send them to *zauthor@zondervan.com*.

With Zondervan: Submit your review of this book by writing to *zreview@zondervan.com*.

Free Online Resources at
www.zondervan.com

Zondervan AuthorTracker: Be notified whenever your favorite authors publish new books, go on tour, or post an update about what's happening in their lives at www.zondervan.com/authortracker.

Daily Bible Verses and Devotions: Enrich your life with daily Bible verses or devotions that help you start every morning focused on God. Visit www.zondervan.com/newsletters.

Free Email Publications: Sign up for newsletters on Christian living, academic resources, church ministry, fiction, children's resources, and more. Visit www.zondervan.com/newsletters.

Zondervan Bible Search: Find and compare Bible passages in a variety of translations at www.zondervanbiblesearch.com.

Other Benefits: Register to receive online benefits like coupons and special offers, or to participate in research.